AF237637

In memory of Sr. Sigmunda May

Christina Mülling
Paul Zahner

Franciscan School

of Prayer

bibliographic data are available on the Internet via
<http://dnb.ddb.de>.

1st edition 2022

© Christina Mülling

Production and publishing: BoD – Books on Demand, Norderstedt

ISBN 978-3-7543-0715-1

Grafikdesign Cover: Sr. Anna Barbara Regnat,
                    Kloster Sießen

CONTENTS

Preamble 1

Brother Thomas of Celano writes beautifully of St. Francis as someone who was "not so much praying as becoming totally prayer."[1] This small *Book of Prayer* may help us to experience that transformation, as we move from the words of prayer to those words being made flesh in our everyday experience. Like Francis, we may move from one form of prayer to another at various moments in our lives. The young Francis composed prayers full of requests for himself: "enlighten the darkness of *my* heart," "give *me* true faith, certain hope, and perfect charity, ... sense and knowledge." In his middle years, now surrounded by brothers and sisters, his prayer changed to include them: "'Your kingdom come': that You may rule in *us* through Your grace, and enable *us* to come to Your kingdom."[2] Toward the end of his life, even in a time of darkness and suffering, his prayer changes again, to focus entirely on his Beloved: "*You* are our hope, *You* are our faith, *You* are our charity."[3]

In the pages that follow, the reader will find forms of prayer adapted to the changing circumstances of our lives. Some of these engage the mind in quiet reflection on the Word of God, while others fix our gaze on a sacred image. Here one will find ways of praying adapted to the busy moments of the workday and to calm times of sabbath rest. Keeping our focus on the Beloved Son, we are encouraged to pray by engaging ourselves completely: body and soul, heart and mind, emotions and imagination. The whole person prays, and in that process, over time, the whole person is transfigured into the Image of God seen in Christ and in ourselves, members of His Body.

---

[1] 2C 95 in FA:ED II:310.
[2] PrOF 4 in FA:ED I:158.
[3] PrG 6 in FA:ED I:109.

1

The depth of St. Clare's expressions of loving attention to the presence of Christ around her teach us to "gaze, consider, contemplate, desiring to imitate" our loving Spouse. She shows us the way to fix our attention on a holy image dear to us, and to recognize the presence of Christ in the sick and suffering. We can find in her twords and example a spiritual guide, a "soul-friend," who loved her own soul and the souls of her sisters, encouragin us to do the same.

Francis and Clare chose the path of poverty and humility because they recognized it as the path taken by the Beloved Son. Following His footprints, they cared for the sick, the poor and the abandoned, who found in them both loving care and healing. They gladly performed the work of servants for their brothers and sisters, as Jesus had done for the people of His day. And like His disciples, they recognized Him as the Risen One in the "breaking of the bread."[4] For them, and for us, no clearer sign of the "humility of God" can be found than the "ordinary piece of bread,"[5] in which Christ in the Eucharist "is always with His faithful."[6]

In the various sections of this book, we can discover the complex contours and textures of that "spirit of holy prayer and devotion"[7] which all our work must serve, desiring above all else to have "the Spirit of the Lord and its holy activity."[8] Here we can find heart-felt meditations on the mysteries of Mary, mother of the Lord, "the virgin made Church."[9] We retrace through affection and imagination the steps of the suffering Christ along the Way of the Cross. We are surrounded by many brothers and sisters,

---

[4] Lk 24:35.
[5] LtOrd 27 in FA:ED I:118.
[6] Adm I:22 in FA:ED I:129.
[7] LR V:2 in FA:ED I:102.
[8] LR X:8 in FA:ED I:105.
[9] SalBVM 1 in FA:ED I:163.

the creatures that show us the loving care of their Creator.[10] Even in suffering and illness or awaiting our "Sister Death", we can still give praise and bless the Most High "and serve Him with great humility."[11]

May the words of this book spark in your heart a warm flame of love for the Word made flesh. May you find here a renewed love for our Sister Mother Earth and all God's creation. May you learn to delight in contemplating the image of God's Beloved in yourself and in those around you. And may we all learn in our prayer to be grateful for everything to the One who is "the fulness of good, all good, every good, the true and supreme good, Who alone is good."[12]

Our gratitude begins by expressing thanks to the authors of this volume for making available to us today the treasures of Francis, "the Little Poor Man", and the beauty of Clare, the "little plant" of this garden of God.

Br. William J. Short, O.F.M.

Rome

Solemnity of the Epiphany 2021

---

[10] CantC 10-14 in FA:ED I:114.

[11] CantC 10-14 in FA:ED I:114.
[12] ER XXIII:9 in FA:ED I:85.

Preamble 2

Dear Sisters and Brothers!
Dear friends interested in Franciscan spirituality and
Franciscan life!

For many years, the group "Contemplative Path" met mainly in the convent of the Franciscan Sisters in Siessen to deepen appreciation for the treasure and wisdom of Franciscan Spirituality and Contemplation. Unfortunately, they do not meet anymore at present, although some members are still interested in continuing to deepen this subject together. Emerging from the "Contemplative Path", the "Franciscan School of Prayer", introduced people to contemplation in Siessen for many years.

The aim of the School of Prayer is to show a path that leads, step by step, into the depths of prayer, and seeks to pass on the wisdom and tradition of Franciscan contemplation, in a contemporary context. The following texts can be used, as originally intended, as a personal school of prayer with daily meditations (30 minutes) for one week, or they can simply be used as individual elements for personal meditation. Some of these texts offer brief information on important aspects of Franciscan spirituality, and thus introduce people to concrete themed spirituality. Originally the texts of the prayer schools started with the first week of Advent and lasted from Lent until about Pentecost (approx. December to May). However, they can also be used independent of the liturgical season.

We especially thank the following Franciscan Sisters of Siessen for their collaboration during the development of the School of Prayer in Siessen and in the draft of the presented texts: Sr. M. Judith Jung OSF, Sr. M. Brigitte Wahl OSF and Sr. Claudia-Maria Mühlherr OSF.

We sincerely wish you fruitful meditations, a deep enthusiasm for God's mysteries and a patient persistence in contemplation.

Special thanks go to Ms. Maria Struckmann-Haszler, Sr. Claudia Maria Mühlherr OSF, Sr. M. Sophia Gisa OSF and Ms. Barbara Thomas for translation, and Ms. Natalia Haszler for editing.

Together with Francis from the bottom of our hearts we wish you: "May the Lord give you peace!" (Dominus det tibi pacem!).

Fr. Paul Zahner OFM (Zurich)
Sr. M. Christina Mülling OSF (Wurzburg)

Franciscan Contemplation – Introduction

The method, the active practice of Franciscan con-emplation, is embedded in God's action of grace. God gives Himself and in doing so, transforms the human heart. Only within the "context" of God's surrender to me, am I able to surrender in prayer.

I. Let God gaze at you

- In front of the cross of San Damiano, Francis experienced that he was gazed upon and addressed by the Lord.

- Appear before Jesus Christ externally and internally *(the San Damiano Cross or any other image of Jesus can be of help)* and become aware that Jesus is looking at you, addressing you, touching you.
  Let him gaze at you, address you and touch you.
  Let him perceive you.
  He seeks a home, a dwelling in you.

- Then look yourself into the mirror of the Divine Reality, into the mirror of Jesus.
  St. Clare describes this gaze in her second letter to St. Agnes of Prague (2LAg 20) in three words:

II. Look, hear, touch

1. Perceiving (latin: intuere)
Now look at Him, who is looking at you. Look for Him, who is looking for you (see Gen 16:13). Carefully, blinking first. Then with open eyes. Look, read, let him meet you. Become "aware" of Him.

2. Considering (latin: considerare)

Now come closer to His mystery. Try to understand, to ponder, to roll back and forth, to ruminate, to read repeatedly. Again and again move towards Him and His mystery. Consider the fullness of His diversity. Be aware of Him.

3. Contemplating (latin: contemplare)

Let all considerations go. Look at him. He is looking at you. His gaze is resting on you. Let your eyes rest on Him. Look at Him. Enter the mystery of His presence. Prepare a "home and dwelling place for Him".

III. Being touched and transformed

Let your perception go, let yourself be perceived, let yourself be taken up by Him.
Try not to look or seek to understand, but let yourself be involved. Let go, because He wants to change, to transform you.

"No longer I live, but Christ lives in me" (Gal 2:19).
HE transforms what HE has taken as His home and dwelling place.

1. God's Longing – Practising Franciscan contemplation

1. The quest for meaning and longing as the starting point of all human paths

The central motive of all who search and who pray is the longing of the soul for its origin. We all feel deep in our hearts the inner compass, seeking for a place where we can be whole, healed and one. Yet the compass of "longing" does not guarantee arrival at the destination. Human beings experience themselves in their longing, but are often misguided and painfully incapable of finding the correct path. God himself speaks into this powerlessness, in many different ways and always anew: in his word and sacrament, in disappointments ... Mechthild of Magdeburg, a medieval German mystic, testifies from her experience of God: *"God has enough of all things, only the touch of the soul never becomes enough for him."*

2. Francis and Clare as human beings who long for God

More than anything else, Francis and Clare were human beings full of longing. In fact, the word longing is a key word of Franciscan-Clarian spirituality. Francis tirelessly reminds his brothers to want nothing else but God alone, to give priority to the keen search for the Kingdom of God in their own lives.

Clare also gives the ardent longing for the poor Christ Crucified the absolute priority in her life. Building on this emphasis of God's longing in Clare and Francis, the Franciscan brother, Bonaventure (†1274), later describes a spiritual path to the mystery of God, which originates and is continuously driven by the Longing for God: *"No one is even somehow disposed for God-given contemplation, which leads to an ecstasy of the spirit, if he is not like Daniel a ·man of longing'. But longing can be inflamed in us in two ways:*

by the loud calling in prayer ... and by the illuminating splendour during contemplation" (Itinerarium, Prologue 3). For Bonaventure, longing itself is the path to God.

However, from the Franciscan perspective, the longing of the human being for God is only a reaction to the much deeper longing of God for human beings. Francis is amazed that it is God's longing to create *"a home and dwelling place"* in human hearts (2LtF 48) and to make them the betrothed of Jesus Christ. Clare cannot believe that it is God's longing to find a home in the faithful soul (3LAg 21-22). The great Franciscan theologian John Duns Scotus (†1308) even develops a whole theology of God's longing. He suggests that the Triune God created creation unnecessarily, because He Himself is the fulfilment of all longing, nevertheless God's foolish love grew and pushed beyond its own limits. Through the creation of man, God wanted to create creatures as beings, who love together with him. It is God's incredible longing to give himself to human beings and to live with them. A human being's longing to be with God is the answer to God's longing to dwell in the human being. The beginning of the contemplative path of human beings with God is always their amazement at God's longing.

3. God's Longing – a lifelong process of transformation

In the writings of Francis and Clare it becomes clear how great the passion was with which they fought for themselves and for their brothers and sisters, subordinating all their wishes, needs and desires to God's longing.

They understood maturing in God's longing as a lifelong contemplative process with continuous willingness to repent and to suffer "for the love to the love". Tirelessly they encourage and admonish us to advance on the path of choosing poverty, humble patience and to reveal the distress of temptations and tiredness (acedia in Latin) to brothers/sisters, so that "help" can be found.

The prayers of St. Francis give us a sense of the spiritual struggle in his longing for God – for example in the "Praise of La Verna" or in the "Meditation to the Lord's Prayer" ... In the Earlier Rule, in chapter 23, Francis presents to his brothers the only desirable good, and expands on how this longing can be accorded concrete space in their lives. He points out that at the end of the day, nothing, no existential needs and nothing which separates or falsifies, should be an obstacle to holding on to the highest good in one's heart.

Francis appeals passionately:

"Let us all love the Lord God Who has given and gives to each one of us our whole body, our whole soul and our whole life, Who has created, redeemed and will save us by His mercy alone, Who did and does everything good for us, miserable and wretched, rotten and foul, ungrateful and evil ones. We do not want to desire, to wish anything else, nothing else shall please and delight us as our Creator and Redeemer and Savior, the only true God, who is the fullness of the good, all the good, the whole good, the true and the highest good who alone is good ... So nothing should hinder us, nothing separate, nothing should interfere.
Everywhere, anywhere, every hour and anytime, daily and incessantly, we all want to truly and humbly believe in Him and hold on to Him in our hearts, to love, honor, worship, serve, praise and bless, glorify and exalt Him, laude and give thanks to Him, the most solemn and highest everlasting God, the Trinity and Oneness, the Father and the Son and the Holy Spirit, the Creator of all and the Savior of all who believe in Him and hope for Him and love Him, Who is without beginning and without an end, invariable, invisible, indescribable, inexpressible, incomprehensible, inscrutable, praised, worthy of glory, glorious, exalted, dear, solemn, sweet, lovable, delightful and highly desirable above all from eternity to eternity. Amen" (ER 23:8-11).

St. Bonaventure shows in his "Pilgrimage of the Soul to God" (Itinerarium) how change should take place. Not those one who think and study a lot will find God, but they who seek him longingly. However, if someone thinks longingly, as Bonaventura does, this way of thinking will help a lot on his way towards God.

At the end of his work, Bonaventura sums up his approach on how the mystery of transformation in the encounter with God should happen in the following concise words:

"If you now ask how this should happen, then ask grace, not doctrine, the longing, not knowledge, the sigh of prayer, not the eager reading, the bridegroom, not a teacher, God, not a human, darkness, not clarity, not the light, but the fire that inflames completely, and that by unspeakable anointing and glowing movement of the heart transfers into God. This fire is God, 'whose furnace is in Jerusalem' (Is 31:9), and Christ has inflamed it in the glow of His burning passion" (Itinerarium VII:6).
(Bonaventure, Der Pilgerweg des Menschen zu Gott, translated and explained by Marianne Schlosser, St. Ottilien 2010, 105.)

4. Exercise

Choose between the text of Bonaventure and the prayer of Francis:

> ➤ First, gather yourself, be aware of his gaze and receive his longing trustingly.

> ➤ Then, read repeatedly the text of St. Bonaventure (or St. Francis) and perceive how it reshapes your thinking. Seek Him, seek the one who is seeking you longingly. Give this inner movement space.

➢ Look back at yourself with His longing gaze, entrust yourself to Him; let a prayer of the heart rise up, and remain in His presence.

➢ During this week, write your own prayer of longing, which expresses your painful process of wishes, needs, longings, and your hope in Him.

2. Living out of the word of God – receiving his gaze through the living word

Introduction

I gather myself with the impulse:
Your Word gives me ... strength ... confidence ...
What is my approach to the holy Scriptures?
What significance does the Bible have in my life?
What do I desire for myself?

1. Francis and the living Word

Francis knew about the life-giving power of the Word of God, about its power that connects to the innermost Life of God, and about its indispensable fruitfulness with regard to love. Therefore, he confesses faithfully in the letter to the clerics: *"For we have and see nothing bodily of the Most High in this world except His Body and Blood, His names and words through which we have been made and redeemed from death to life" (LtCl 3).*

This compilation: The Sacrament of the Holy Eucharist and the Word of God seem to be daring for many, even after the Second Vatican Council. We do believe that God is present in the Sacrament, but to accept it in the same way for the Word, does not seem so familiar to us. Francis perceives the powerful healing efficacy of the Word of God and the Sacrament as one, because in both of them, Christ, the Word of the Father, comes to us to redeem us (as in the Letter to the Faithful, 2LtF 4-15).

In this we actually meet him in a real way, or as Francis says, "bodily". Holy Scripture therefore not only gave him testimony from God that it was good for man to read; but, as Francis expressly confesses, it is "to seek the Lord our God" (2C 105:3) and therefore also to be found. Therefore, the Holy Bible not only bore witness to God, being good for man to read; but in it, as Francis explicitly confesses, "the Lord our God is to be sought" (2C 105:3) and therefore also to be found.

Francis speaks of the *"contemplating the Holy Gospel"* (ER 1:1). It is first of all a precise perception, a form of observation, which then leads to imitation, following and practising what one has perceived. In order to try it myself, according to this example and to imitate Him, I must contemplate the Lord and Master Jesus Christ Himself and observe Him closely, as, for example, at the Last Supper, when he washes the feet of His disciples one after the other (Jn 13:14f). Francis *"recalls with regular meditation the words of Christ"* (1C 84). Brother Thomas uses the Latin verb "recordari" for the English word "remember", which means "to heed again".

2. The contemplation of the Holy Bible according to Francis

The contemplation of the incarnate Word of God has something to do with the heart. It is an activity "which recalls the words and works of Christ in the heart or rediscovers them" (Johannes Schneider, Gottes-Sehnsucht, p. 55). It is necessary to turn to the Holy Bible with your heart (not with your mind!), in compliance with the words of the psalm: You have said, "Seek my face. My heart says to you, 'Your face, Lord, do I seek'" (Ps 27:8). It is about a living encounter with Him, a time of lingering in the Word that "has become flesh". He wants to show Himself to me, to talk to me, to allow me to understand better.

Francis cultivated a *"shared communion"* (Johannes Schneider) with the Word of God in the sense of John's Gospel: *"If anyone loves me, he will keep my word, and my Father will love him, and we will come to him and make our home with him"* (Jn 14:23). Christ is "the Image of God", the Image of the invisible God. By looking at Christ lovingly, we experience with our hearts and minds what it means that he is the Path to the Father. He will introduce us to His relationship with the Father, and we will gain a home in the Triune Community of Love.

The purpose of this week's input is to work on the living encounter with Christ in His Word. The scriptural texts are the ones of the current readings of the Eucharist in the Catholic Church.

3. Exercise

A) Contemplation of the Gospel of the Day in three steps:

1. I start by perceiving myself physically and "gathering" myself. Then I call upon the Holy Spirit. I realize that the gaze of Christ is upon me. I join His gaze: How are You, Jesus, looking at me today?

2. I read the text of the Gospel of the Day. I look at Him through the "eyes of the heart", I look at Him in the current situation, which is described in the corresponding verse. I try to understand what is going on, why He behaves as he does, etc. In doing so, I constantly repeat the verse or verses I am attracted to.

3. I let go of all considerations and start to look only at Him while staying in His living presence. I let myself be captivated by His will. I end the contemplation by discussing with Jesus how I want to follow Him today. I summarize this in a short prayer.

4. To recognize the guidance of God in my life, the following can be helpful:

- Write down the key verse or what you want to live by today, after a time of contemplation. After the time of contemplation, note the key verse or note what you want to put into practice in writing.

- In the evening, report to yourself and God how you have dealt with your verse throughout the day.

- From time to time, read the notes on your respective contemplations and become aware of the central theme of God's guidance in His Word.

B) Praying the Rosary of the Scripture (according to Johannes Schneider, Gottes-Sehnsucht, p. 68ff)

The Rosary of the Scripture is especially suitable for a phase of intensification, in which you repeat the key verses of your contemplation, in which I repeat the Word (see point 2 above). Together with Mary, treasure up and ponder "all words in the heart" (Luke 2:19). If you pray it in the context of contemplation, use the vocation prayer as an opening prayer for the entire contemplation.

Opening: *Prayer of* *St. Francis for* *enlightenment of* *the heart*	Most High, glorious God, enlighten the darkness of my heart and give me true faith, certain hope, and perfect charity, sense and knowledge, Lord, that I may carry out Your holy and true command. Amen.
First half of *the* *"Ave Maria"*	Hail, Mary, full of grace, the Lord is with thee. Blessed art thou among women, and blessed is the fruit of thy womb, Jesus:

Here I insert a verse from the Gospel, which I repeat 7-10 times, depending on the count	*(Example from the Monday of the 2nd week of Advent:)* "Jesus, who says: Get up and go!"
Second half of the "Ave Maria"	Holy Mary, Mother of God, pray for us sinners, now and at the hour of our death. (Amen.)

Continuation with the 2nd law:

First half of the "Ave Maria"	Hail Mary, full of grace, the Lord is with thee, blessed art thou among women, and blessed is the fruit of thy womb, Jesus:
Second verse to repeat 7-10 times	"Jesus, who heals in the power of the Lord" or "Jesus, forgiving all sins"
Second half of the "Ave Maria"	Holy Mary, Mother of God, pray for us sinners, now and at the hour of our death. (Amen.)

etc.

3. Holistic prayer – The State of Praying

Introduction

I collect myself and make myself aware: Is there a posture of prayer that I particularly like to pray in?

- in personal prayer
- in the Eucharist
- in the contemplation of the Word of God
- in looking at the prayer of Jesus

1. Finding a holistic way of prayer – to perceive and express one's state of praying

- Every inner emotion desires to be physically expressed. All movements of the heart – such as joy, suffering, love, regret, anger, grief, defense ... – seek their corresponding physical form. Also, faith, hope and love, which are involved in the relationship of prayer, are never just mental-spiritual movements; they express themselves in signs and gestures: The state of praying thus "materializes".

- Already in the initial phase of our explicit time of prayer a great amount of attentiveness is needed to find the true state of prayer, which means that our mental-spiritual state, attitude, and physical condition are consistent in expression and support each other.

- In his guides to prayer, Anthony de Mello emphasizes the incorporation of the body as particularly helpful: *"Stand in front of Him or sit down or kneel down before Him with piously folded hands for prayer. In other words, express with your body the pious reverence that you would like to feel in His presence, but do not feel in the moment of drought and half-heartedness. You will most likely notice that very soon your heart and mind express what your body expresses. You will feel His presence more clearly, and your tired heart will warm. This is the great advantage of praying with the body. I do not just have a body; I am my body."*

- Regarding the holistic form of prayer, the instruction to *Ignatian Prayer states: "Entering contemplation by kneeling, stretched out on the ground, on one's back with one's face up, by sitting, standing; while always seeking for what I want."* This "what I want" is not so much a matter of the mind, but rather of where I want to be while following the promptings of the Holy Spirit. Therefore, it is important to enter the time of prayer with care, cautiousness and concentration to find presence in the state of prayer, and then to stay in it.

2. Finding the inner form of prayer

Every form of prayer (whether verbal, meditative or contemplative prayer) is ultimately about "inner prayer". This is not a level of prayer, but an inner attitude, which is the basis and support for all prayer and embraces the person as a whole. Inner prayer directs a loving form of attention towards God – an awareness of His presence and his constant willingness to be in relationship with us human beings is a loving attention directed to God – an awareness of His presence and constant willingness to relate to us human beings. Inner prayer works in two ways: the praying person has an idea of the contrast between divine perfection and one's own brokenness in being human. But one also feels God's greatness and the all-embracing love in which one knows oneself to be completely and eternally accepted and safe.

3. The holistic way of praying of Francis and Clare

Brother Thomas of Celano writes:

- *"A pilgrim while in the body, away from the Lord, Francis, the man of God, strove to keep himself present in spirit to heaven, ... With all his soul he thirsted for his Christ: To him he dedicated not only his whole heart but also his whole body ... When it happened that he was suddenly overcome in public by a visitation of the Lord so as not to be without a cell, he would make a little cell out of his mantle..." (2C 94).*

- *"But when praying in the woods or solitary places he would fill the forest with groans, water the places with tears, strike his breast with his hand, and, as if finding a more secret hiding place, he often conversed out loud with his Lord. ... He would often ruminate inwardly with unmoving lips, and, drawing outward things inward, he raised his spirit to the heights. Thus, he would direct all his attention and affection toward the one thing he asked of the Lord, not so much praying as totally becoming prayer." (2C 95).*

- Francis finds his most intense form of identity in prayer. This can also be noticed linguistically: every time he pronounces *"God"* or *"Jesus"*, his language rises to a poetic form of expression and prayer. He lives in a constant readiness for prayer, in an attitude that easily turns into ecstatic forms of expression. Francis is very versatile in his prayers, both in terms of content and in terms of his expression: He praises, thanks, adores, remains silent, ruminates (repeated praying), hums melodies ... He involves the body in focused sitting, standing, walking, kneeling, lying, bent towards the ground, stretched out in the shape of a cross ...
Before his stigmatization in 1224, for example, he prays on the mountain of La Verna for a long time with outstretched arms: *"Who are you, loving God – who am I, little worm, your little servant"* (see Rotzetter / Dijk / Matura: Franz von Assisi, No. 43/44).

4. Practising my own state of prayer

A)

➤ I pause in the place where I pray.

➤ With a wide gesture I take a focused posture, possibly my favorite posture for praying.

> By conscious breathing, I gradually feel through the individual parts of my body and perceive possible tensions or relaxation ("feeling" not thinking!).

> Listening to my breath, I let myself be guided deeper and deeper towards the center of myself, through current conflicts, afflictions ...

B)

> I keep silent and listen, trying to perceive if a suppressed cry, which wants to be physically expressed, announces itself. This is my state of prayer.

> These ascending calls can also be expressed through words of the Holy Bible such as:
"My soul thirsts for you!"
"You have prepared a body for me. Behold, I come to do your will."
"Lord, Jesus Christ, have mercy on me."
"I praise you Father, Lord of Heaven and Earth ..."

C)
> I sense the gesture that corresponds to what I have recognized in my prayer and what I want to implement in my everyday life.

5. A relaxation exercise in especially stressful situations

Arriving	I have time, I take a seat and calm down.
Feeling one's body	I perceive the way I am sitting, how the chair and floor carry me.

I settle down and straighten up from
the inside.
My hands are resting in my lap,
my eyes half open looking towards
the ground.

Relaxation of the body	I relax my body from the center down and upwards. While inhaling I sense the parts of my body, while exhaling I relax.

*Relaxation of
the body*

I relax my body
from the center down and upwards.
While inhaling I sense the parts of
my body, while exhaling I relax.

Breathing

I listen into my breath,
how it comes, how it goes
and exhale everything stressful.

*Relaxation of
the will*

I let go of all pressure and self-will
I do not need to show off,
to achieve or to perform anything.

*Relaxation of
the spirit*

Now, I relax my mind.
Everything can be as it is:
my state of being,
my thoughts and feelings,
people, sounds ...
I do not hold anything; I let
everything go –
also, resistances and inner
oppositions,
temptations, weariness ...

*To be awake
and open in the
presence of
God*

I am fully present
and perceive His presence in faith.
I present to Him "what I want".
I listen to the call of my heart,
the sighing of the spirit,
that wants to rise ...

That is how I open myself up
for the threefold mystery,
which is present in my depths –
Him, the very other ...

Letting it   To be there in His presence, in His
happen to me   gaze – gazing – to remain silent ...
gazing back.
Feeling which form of Christ
what Word of God desires to grow
within me.
(for example, Jesus Christ, the
praying person – the Healer – the
One who is raised up – the one
who was crucified and abandoned
– the one who is risen)
Perceiving how the love of the
Father rests on Jesus,
that is how it rests on me, too.

Concluding   Give thanks as a whole person, as
Francis says, "to return everything
good!"
"Stay in my love!"

4. Incarnation – Allowing the birth of God within Myself

Introduction

I carefully prepare myself to be introduced to the topic of this week. I let my most existential, deepest wish for Christmas rise within myself. Do I find my most precious wish in a Christmas carol, a prayer, a written word or a poem?

1. The image of God according to St. Francis

Francis admires and contemplates three mysteries of the life of Jesus incessantly: the humble descent of God into our flesh and blood in the incarnation of Jesus (the Nativity); the humble and patient descent of Jesus into the darkest depths of our lives in His suffering until death on the cross, and the humble devotion of Jesus to man in the Eucharist. He kneels adoringly before the Eucharistic Bread, he reads compassionately in the "Book of the Cross of Christ" day and night, he looks in amazement at and yearns for the mystery of the incarnation of God in our hearts, in his own heart.

In this approach, two attitudes of Jesus have become especially important to Francis: the "humilitas" = humility and the "patientia" = patience. In the incarnation of Jesus, he discovers the humilitas, the approach to humus, the earth, meaning, the humble humiliation of God. In the Passion, the patient suffering, the patientia of God, with the aim of bringing man lovingly back home into the communion with God.

In the Second Letter to the Faithful, Francis states that the humilitas of Jesus was accepting through the womb of Mary the very flesh of our humanity and fragility (2LtF 2:4). Jesus accepted humanity not only in its beautiful, but also in its fragile reality. Francis uses three concepts in his writings to describe this reality: "fragilitas" (fragility, frailty, weakness), "debilitas" (paralysis, frailty) and "infirmitas" (illness, powerlessness, lack of talent, weakness of character, inconstancy, timidity, lack of independence, unreliability). Therefore, it really is a comprehensive acceptance of our fragility. Jesus accepted our fragility so that we could meet Him in our fragility and find healing, deliverance and reconciliation in him.

At La Verna, the high point of his life, Francis finally realizes that God Himself is humilitas and patientia. When he prays in the Praise of God, *"You are the humility! You are the patience!" (The Praises of God 4)* – then these are the qualities of the Father, which became visible in Jesus. *"He who sees me sees the Father!"* Therefore, God Himself shines through in the humble descent and suffering patience of Jesus. Thus, the humilitas and the patientia are not only preconditions for relating to God, but God Himself is humility and patience. The humble and patient man is already in God, he already has a share in God: you in me and me in you!

2. Incarnation – the birth of God inside of us

In Jesus, God bends down into the darkest depths of human existence, to bring everything which is lost back home to His love. But even more than that, Jesus does not simply descend to a level of human equality, he goes even lower through the cross, with this he takes the very last, lowest human position. He, God Himself, makes Himself the very last of mankind. What humility, what patience!

For us humans that means specifically: God is waiting for us in the abyss of our life, our heart is the place of the incarnation within us. Therefore, the Franciscan way of unification with God also leads downwards, into one's own fragility, into one's brokenness and into the brokenness of our community. It is a descent into one's own truth, into one's own impotence and therefore onto a path of humility. Thus, it is not about eradicating, about getting rid of everything that does not fit the picture which I would like to have of myself. It is about bringing everything which lives and lurks in the dark of my heart into light, to bring it on board, so to speak and then to bring it into contact with the humble and patient Jesus, with His wounds, and this way to let it be transformed, let it change this way.

The Franciscan heaven begins, so to speak, where I myself am, where our community is sinful, weak and fragile before God, and where we ask for His mercy. So, He can become flesh and blood in our own hearts.

3. Francis sees an analogy between the Incarnation and the Eucharist

Finally, Francis discovers these two attitudes even in the Eucharist, in the bread that is broken for us. In the first exhortation he writes (Adm 1:16): *"Look, daily He lowers Himself"* – in the original text it actually means: He humbles Himself – *"as He once came down from the royal throne into the womb of the Virgin."*

In one breath, Francis names the mystery of incarnation and the Eucharist. He sees the celebration of the Eucharist as the ongoing incarnation in time. St. Bonaventure pursues this idea when he writes:

"For us He exudes himself, unites us and transforms us in Himself, through the fiery love through which He gave Himself to us (in the Incarnation), for us (in the Crucifixion), gave back again to us (in the Eucharist), and remains with us until the end of the world" (Breviloquium VI:9).

4. Succeeding means allowing the birth of God

The answer of man to the experienced humility of God can therefore be for Francis only to follow Christ in this humility and devotion. Francis thus discovers the deeply lowered, humble God in the very poor child in the manger, in the suffering Christ on the cross and in the Eucharist. Where Christ is, Francis also wants to be. He wants to descend into His humility and patience in order to share his life with Him, to become more and more like Him through imitation, as Paul says: *"No longer I live, but Christ lives in me!"*

Francis is convinced that through the humble and patient attitude of life, man is given community and unity with the Divine Trinity. Thus Francis writes in a letter to the faithful (2LtF 48): *"And the Spirit of the Lord will rest upon all those men and women who have done and persevered in these things and It will make a home and dwelling place in them"* (Jn 14:23).

5. Exercise

In the breathing prayer, I can practise joining the descent of Jesus (exhaling) and the ascent of the risen Christ (inhaling).

- ➢ I invite Jesus to come to me in my concrete fragility and to take shape within me. I perceive the longing, the sighing of the Spirit inside me.

- ➢ In the rhythm of my breath, I descend with Jesus into my brokenness – through the layers of resistance and pain. In the process, I ask for patient acceptance and perseverance. While breathing in, I hope for new life out of Christ and open myself to the people who are in my life.

- ➢ At the lowest point, I let myself be taken with Jesus to the Father and let myself be transformed. Continue with this basic orientation and try to live in redeeming joy in everyday life.

5. Preparing a Mansion and Dwelling for him

I. Like Mary

Introduction

This week, we contemplate the mystery of the incarnation of the Son of God in the spirit of St. Francis. His *"Salutation to the Blessed Virgin Mary"* and the icon *"Mother of God of the Sign"* are intended to be a bridge for us, to guide us into the fundamental calling of every Christian.

I gather myself through the prayer of Pope John XXIII:

"Grace my heart, Lord,
with Your presence,
turn it into a dwelling place for You!

You are the guest I expect
the friend who should stay with me.
You, who deserve a palace,
I have only a poor hut to offer.

I grace my heart
with longing and desire.
Then the brightness of the sky
will brighten my home.
My house – the cathedral,
My heart – the tabernacle.

Grace my heart, Lord,
with Your presence,
turn it into a dwelling place for You!"

1. Some hints on the type of the icon "Our Lady of the Sign"

"Our Lady of the Sign", Sr. Maria Francesca Hofer OSF
© Tertiarschwestern Brixen, based on a Russian icon, late 16th century

This icon is based on the verse by Isaiah 7:14: *"Therefore the Lord himself will give you a sign. Behold, the virgin shall conceive and bear a son, and shall call his name Immanuel – God with us."*

Considering this promise, an icon with the name *"Znamenie" – "Our Lady of the Sign"* was written in the Eastern Church. Its prototype was kept in the "Blachernen Church" in Constantinople. Icono-graphically, this type can be traced back to the 9th century. In this icon, one can see a close match between the image and its name.

Immediately we notice the strong centering of the image, which draws us into it. The emphasized center gathers and unites our painfully divergent tendencies. Mary appears in the Orante posture, the prayer posture of ancient time – a position of waiting, completely focused on the fulfillment of the promise. The color of the garment of the Mother of God is identified as brown purple. Brown is the color of the earth, purple is the color of saintliness, of royalty. In Mary, heaven and earth are connected. The head and shoulders of Christ "Immanuel" hover on an aureole on her breast. The majestic Christ emerges from the circle. His right hand is raised as a sign of God's faithfulness to the covenant, his left hand holds the scroll, a symbol of the eternal word that comes from the Father. At the same time Immanuel is carried by the seraphim, "the burning one" in bright red (see Isa 6:26). It is a reference to the holiness of God present in Jesus incarnate. He is an indication of the holiness of God's presence in Jesus Incarnate.

The icon "Our Lady of the Sign" is preferably depicted on the "diskos", the altar on which the offerings for the Eucharist are prepared. This is a reference to the coming of Immanuel to us, as once in the womb of the Blessed Mother. In many hymns this mystery is sung, especially during Christmas time. For Francis it becomes an experience of prayer.

2. Being like Mary – the fundamental calling of a Christian

In analogy to the Mother of God, Francis regards the Christian as a person who has become *"his home and dwelling place"* (1LtF 6) through the Spirit of the Lord and is called *"to always make, a home and a dwelling place there for Him"* (ER 22:27) and at the same time to live in communion with the Trinity.

The heart is the living temple in which love, the relationship between God and man, grows. The Virgin Mary is the role model of those who accept the Word of God, keep it in their inner cell of silence and live it day by day.

In the Letter to the Faithful, Francis turns passionately to all women and men who *"hate their wrong self"* and *"love the Lord with all their hearts... and their neighbor as themselves."* He unlocks the great promises of the gospel (Mt 12:50; Jn 14:23; Jn 17), which have become a mystical experience for him: *"O how happy and blessed are these men and women while they do such things and persevere in doing them, because the Spirit of the Lord will rest upon them and make Its home and dwelling place among them, and they are children of the heavenly Father Whose works they do, and they are spouses, brothers, and mothers of our Lord Jesus Christ.*

We are spouses when the faithful soul is joined by the Holy Spirit to our Lord Jesus Christ. We are brothers to Him when we do the will of the Father who is in heaven. We are mothers when we carry Him in our heart and body through a divine love and a pure and sincere conscience and give birth to Him through a holy activity which must shine as an example before others" (1LtF 1:5-10).

3. The "Salutations to the Blessed Virgin Mary" (SalBVM) by St. Francis

In the "Salutations to the Mother of God" the experience of St. Francis became a prayer:

[1] Hail, O Lady,
Holy Queen,
Mary, holy Mother of God,
Who are the Virgin made Church,
[2] chosen by the most Holy Father in heaven
whom he consecrated with His most holy beloved Son
and with the Holy Spirit the Paraclete,
[3] in whom there was and is
all fullness of grace and every good.

[4] Hail to His Palace!
Hail to His Tabernacle!

Hail to His Dwelling!
⁵ Hail to His Robe!
Hail to His Servant!
Hail to His Mother!

⁶ And hail to all You holy virtues
which are poured into the hearts of the faithful
through the grace and enlightenment of the Holy Spirit,
that from being unbelievers,
You may make them faithful to God.

4. Understanding the prayer

To understand the prayer, we refer to Father Leonhard Lehmann OFMCap in "Franziskus – Meister des Gebets" (Kevelaer 1989). The Salutation to the Mother of God is divided into three verses, which are again divided into three parts. Apparently here in the form of the greeting, the worship of Francis for the holy Trinity is reflected.

The angel's greeting (Lk 1:28) combined with the Greeting of Elizabeth (Lk 1:42) had been known through the "Ave Maria prayer" since the 7th/8th century. Around 1200, synods began to prescribe the prayer "Ave Maria" following the "Our Father" – at that time without the addition introduced by Bernard of Siena (†1444): *"Holy Mary, Mother of God, pray for us sinners, now and at the hour of our death."* This addition was spread mainly through the introduction of the later Angelus Prayer, which the Franciscans supported.

Francis extends the Salutation of the Angel into a kind of litany of seven Aves. He knows hymns and songs about the motherhood of Mary, but his originality is unmistakable in the additions. Francis "pre-meditates"; thus, the Salutation of the Incarnation of the Son of God in Mary opens into the present: *"In which was and is the fullness of grace"*. Correspondingly, the circle of people widens: What God has done to Mary, he can and wants to do anew through the Holy Spirit. The indwelling of the fullness of God in Mary and the Church is a contemporary event: the fullness

33

of grace, and all goodness relates to all men and all times: to the faithful, whose faith and faithfulness is to mature even more deeply, and to the unbelievers, who shall be present in the yearning of those who pray. Francis prays like a missionary in his adoration of Mary.

5. Exercise

A)

> I give to the icon of *"Our Lady of the Sign"* a befitting place in my room:

> I decorate the space lovingly, including my body and personal prayer attitude, then I enter the space of silence. Gently I empathize with the gesture of Mary and let it become my personal prayer gesture – allowing myself to be looked at. I find my center and my longing together with Mary for the grace to become His dwelling and His home (Jn 14:23).

> Ruminating the *"Salvation to the Mother of God"* to the rhythm of my breathing (praying repeatedly).

> I dedicate myself to the mystery and ask to stay in it during the comings and goings of everyday life.

B)
Praying the Angelus in this contemplative spirit with Francis: During his visit to the Orient, Francis was impressed how the Muslims were called to prayer by the muezzin. Therefore, after his return, he wanted his brothers to invite people to prayer on their missionary trips and to thank God for the Incarnation three times a day. This is another reason why the Catholic tradition of praying the Angelus prayer three times a day developed.
I pray the Angelus, looking internally at the mystery, as a vocational prayer, so that many people can find the

vocation to carry Christ Immanuel within them and testify in the world of today.

II. First Letter to the Faithful

Introduction

In the last years of his life, Francis felt compelled to pass on his spiritual experiences to other people. Thus he wrote many letters. One of them to all faithful Christians. In this letter he develops a deep mysticism of the close love relationship between God and man:

"O how happy and blessed are these men and women while they do such things and persevere in doing them, because the Spirit of the Lord will rest upon them and make Its home and dwelling place among them, (Jn 14:23) and they are children of the heavenly Father Whose works they do, and they are spouses, brothers, and mothers of our Lord Jesus Christ.
We are spouses when the faithful soul is joined by the Holy Spirit to our Lord Jesus Christ. We are brothers to Him when we do the will of the Father who is in heaven. We are mothers when we carry Him in our heart and body through a divine love and a pure and sincere conscience and give birth to Him through a holy activity which must shine as an example before others. O how glorious it is to have a holy and great Father in heaven! O how holy, consoling to have such a beautiful and wonderful Spouse! O how holy and how loving, gratifying, humbling, peace-giving, sweet, worthy of love, and, above all things, desirable: to have such a Brother and such a Son, our Lord Jesus Christ, Who laid down His life for His sheep" (1LtF 5-13).

Exercise

1. Since upon them rests the Spirit of the Lord, and He will make His dwelling and mansion among them (cf. Jn 14:23).

We often strive to make our soul and body a home for the Lord. But God promises us that the Holy Spirit will create His own dwelling and home within us. He acts.

Stay with the sentence: "The Spirit of the Lord rests upon me." Or "The Spirit of the Lord will make His dwelling and home within me." Open yourself to the presence of God in you.

2. We are spouses, when the believing soul is connected to our Lord Jesus Christ through the Holy Spirit.

The term groom, spouse (sponsus) refers to the intimate-loving relationship between the soul of man and Jesus Christ. But I did not become the fiancé(e) of Jesus because I had established this relationship with Jesus Christ myself, but because the Holy Spirit linked me to the Lord.

Dwell on the statement that you, as a spouse, are connected to Jesus Christ through the Holy Spirit. What effect does that have on you?

3. We are His brothers and sisters, when we do *"the Will of the Father who is in Heaven"* (Mt 12:50).

As brothers and sisters of Jesus, we stand at His side. Together with Him, we are sons or daughters of the Heavenly Father. But the will of the Father does not break our own will; it tries to encompass our will. This is exactly what our brother Jesus did, who *"placed His will in the will of His Father"* (2LtF 10).

With something that concerns you, attempt to put your will in the will of the Father in Heaven as we can place our hands in the hands of another person (see the gesture in religious profession, on the hands of the professional sister in the Hands of the mother superior). Or: dwell on the Lord's Prayer: "Thy will be done!" Where do you feel resistance to it?

4. We are mothers, when we carry Him in our hearts and bodies by means of divine love and a pure and sincere conscience; we give birth to Him through holy deeds, which ought to shine as an example for others.

In the unfolding of the gospel (Mt 12:50), Francis tells us that we, as mothers, can give birth to Jesus. Our souls and bodies are involved in the birth.

> *Consider this mystery of the birth of Jesus in your life and the promise that you can be the mother of Jesus. Where do you give birth to Jesus through your being and your behaviour in this world?*

5. O how glorious it is, to have a Holy and Great Father in Heaven! O how holy, consoling, to have such a beautiful and admirable Spouse!

A child is proud when his father is respected and famous. A bride is happy about the handsomeness of her groom. But who could have a greater father and a more beautiful groom than we Christians?

> *As a child, remain conscious of the greatness of your Father in Heaven. Gaze upon God as a woman in love looks at her boyfriend, and let God look at you as a beautiful bride admired by her groom. What do these reflections provoke in you?*

6. O how holy and how beloved, well pleasing, humble, peaceable, sweet, lovable and desirable above all things, to have such a Brother and such a Son: Our Lord Jesus Christ, who laid down His life on behalf of His sheep.
Children trust the strength of an older brother who can free them from any danger. Mothers are proud when their daughters or sons succeed or enjoy a special reputation.

*Keep Jesus in mind like an older brother or follow his
life story with his mother's eyes and heart.
Can you rejoice in his path and be proud of it? What
pleases you particularly at the moment while looking
at the life of Jesus, as described in the Gospels?*

7. Preparing a home and dwelling for Him

*Repeat and deepen one of the exercises or reshape
it as it suits you at the moment.
Or: consider the phrase "home and dwelling place of
God."*

6. Francis tastes the name of Jesus

Introduction

Before we turn to the topic, some introductory questions:

> ➢ My name – what does it mean to me?
> ➢ What do I feel when I am personally addressed with my name?
> ➢ What relationship do I have to the names of other people?
> ➢ The name "Jesus" – what does it mean to me?

1. The worship of the Name of Jesus in history

Although there is great appreciation of the name of Jesus in the Holy Scriptures: *"For no other name under heaven is given to men in whom we are to be saved"* (Acts 4:12), early Christianity did not yet worship of the Name of Jesus. Only in the Middle Ages did popular worship of the name of Jesus develop, especially among the mendicant orders (Cistercians/Bernard of Clairvaux and Dominicans/ Heinrich Seuse). It was prominently promoted by the Franciscans. It reached its peak with Bernard of Siena (†1444) and John Capistrano (†1456), both famous Franciscan itinerant preachers.

Anthony of Padua (†1231), the first teacher of theology for the friars of the Franciscan order, called the name of Jesus *"a name full of loveliness and blessing"* because it reminds us of Christ's salvation act [Jesus (Hebrew) = "Yahweh saves"].

He particularly recommends facing the evil enemy in the power of this name. Also, something similar is reported about St. Bonaventura (†1274).

But the great preacher of the Name of Jesus is Bernard of Siena. In his religious fervour, he also persuaded many priests to place the name of Jesus on the altars or to have them painted on the inner and outer walls of churches.

Also, on public buildings, the name of the Lord was written in capital letters. The abbreviation of the Name of Jesus IHS is provided by him with a memorable content that is often translated into German as: *Jesus, Savior, beatifier.* He has this name made into a radiant symbol. *"That is how I saw the sweet name of our Savior in delight,"* he explains to the people.

*Note to the Name of Jesus (the Monogram of Christ): The short statement "HIS" is derived from the Greek creed "Jesus Christ is the Son of God, the Redeemer" (Jesus Christ, **H**uios Theos, **S**oter). Various (popular) interpretations have arisen from this monogram in Latin:*

- *Jesus Hominum Salvator:* Jesus, Savior of men
- *In hoc salus:* In this is salvation
- *In hoc signo (vinces):* Under this sign (you will be victorious)
- *Iesum Habemus Socium:* We have Jesus as Companion (Society of Jesus / Jesuits)

Monogram on Carceri, photo by Sr. Christina Mülling

40

2. Francis and the Name of Jesus

The Franciscan worship of the Name of Jesus is based on Francis himself, about whom Brother Thomas of Celano says in his first biography (= 1C) from the year 1228/29: *"Whenever he used to say your name, O holy Lord, he was moved in a way beyond human understanding."* Thus he picked up all writings he found lying the ground and laid them in a *"decent place"*, *"because the name of the Lord, or something pertaining to it, might be written there"* (1C 82).

In connection with the celebration of the Nativity in Greccio, we hear the following about Francis: *"Then he preaches to the surrounding people about the birth of the poor king and breaks out in sweet praise of the little town of Bethlehem. Often when he wanted to call Christ 'Jesus', he called him, glowing with over-great love, only 'the Child of Bethlehem', and when he uttered 'Bethlehem' it sounded like a bleating lamb and even more than from his words his mouth overflowed of sweet love"* (1C 86).

In a certain sense, the name of Jesus causes Francis difficulties. As an explanation for this "inhibition of speech", Brother Thomas cites the excessive love that flared up in him through the name of Jesus. He did not have to utter the name of Jesus, it was enough that only wanting to mention the name of Jesus, he was excited by such a great love that it prevented him from uttering the name of the beloved. So he used a paraphrase: *"Child of Bethlehem"*.

His ardent love for Jesus found expression in his body: *"When he mentioned 'Child of Bethlehem' or 'Jesus', he licked his lips as it were, tasting and sipping the sweetness of that name with his blissful palate"* (1C 86). Celano's expression may seem a bit exaggerated. But already with the prophet Jeremiah we find this motive of tasting and devouring the Words and Names of God. *"If words came from You, I devoured them; Your Word was to me happiness and joy of the heart; for Your Name is proclaimed over me, O Lord, God of Armies"* (Jer 15:16). Jeremiah devours the

Words of God like a vital food, joy flows into his heart, because through them the Name of the Lord stands over him, i.e., the Lord Himself becomes present in His Own Name. *"Names and words of God become sacramental signs for the living and loving presence of the Lord. It is this presence of the Lord himself that Francis caresses, tastes, and devours inwardly by mentioning the name of Jesus, like a verbal but real mystical communion"* (Johannes Schneider, Gottes-Sehnsucht, p. 132).

Also in connection with La Verna, Brother Thomas mentions the Holy Name of Jesus Prayer of St. Francis: *"The brothers who lived with him know that daily, constantly, Jesus was always on his lips, sweet and pleasant conversations about Him, kind words full of love. Out of the fullness of his heart his mouth spoke. So the spring of radiant love that filled his heart within gushed forth. He was always with Jesus: Jesus in his heart, Jesus in his mouth, Jesus in his ears, Jesus in his eyes, Jesus in his hands, he bore Jesus always in his whole body"* (1C 115).

3. The meaning of the Holy Name of Jesus Prayer

"To be with Jesus, to be in spiritual communion with him is the real meaning of Jesus' prayer. The everlasting mention of the name of Jesus is communion with the word of God in its densest and most personal form: in its revealed name. Therefore, this form of perpetual prayer encompasses the whole of being. It goes from the lips, which taste the name of Jesus, to the heart, which thus becomes a 'source of enlightened love', fulfills all of its inner emotional world and passes out again into all limbs of the body" (Johannes Schneider, Gottes-Sehnsucht, p.134).

Through the constant loving practice of the Holy-Name-of-Jesus-Prayer, Francis practises the motherly carrying of Jesus within himself, as he emphasizes in the second letter to the faithful: *"(We are) mothers when we carry Him in our heart and body through love and a pure and sincere conscience"* (2LtF 53).

The worship of the Holy Name of Jesus and the practice of the Holy Name of Jesus Prayer belong to the very original forms of Franciscan piety. They will accompany us this week.

Exercises

A) Practising the Jesus Prayer
   (by Emanuel Jungclaussen OSB)

> Find a good sitting position, with an upright posture, hands resting in the lap or on your thighs.

> Turn your attention inwards and become aware of your breath! Let this breath come and go as naturally as possible ... perceive from head to toe: I am here!

> Breathe into the silence, listen to the silence, breathe out into the silence and let the silence become even more intense!

> If you make Jesus' name ring lovingly and with devotion in your heart, then He will be present in the very call of his name. Try it step by step – very intimately, confidingly, tenderly, as you can... "JESUS!"

> Then repeat the name and feel how the name sounds today and right now at this moment! Do not start to ponder or think too much, but rather add boldly, "JESUS CHRIST!"

- ➢ Do not speak the name on your own authority, but feel the other power within you speaking the name though you: "JESUS CHRIST!"

- ➢ All this practice only makes sense if you are ready to serve Him even more, to become a servant of Jesus Christ: "LORD JESUS CHRIST!"

- ➢ All this is a path that lies before you. If you want to advance on it, speak the whole content of the Jesus prayer: "LORD JESUS CHRIST, have mercy on me!"

- ➢ Speak very intimately while inhaling: "LORD JESUS CHRIST" and on exhaling: "have mercy on me!"

- ➢ Repeat the words in the rhythm of your breath for some time, then gradually mute the words of prayer. Let go and listen to the silence while receiving!

- ➢ Then finish the exercise by moving a little back and forth – from right to left, from left to right. Also turn your head a little to the right and to the left! Raise your hands, spread your fingers, then clench your fists to bring some tension into your whole body. Then sit calmly and relaxed, as comfortable as possible.

- ➢ Perhaps this exercise can become a worldwide prayer over the course of this week by formulating: "LORD JESUS CHRIST – HAVE MERCY ON US ALL!"

- ➢ Let all your compassion flow into these words, take all the misfortune and misery of this world and its inhabitants with you to Jesus Christ.

B) Continuation in everyday life – pronounce the name of Jesus over the people

This exercise is suitable as a form of morning prayer in everyday life: The name of Jesus reveals God's love for us human beings and creates new life, true being, the innermost, the hidden, the ultimate reality in each one of us.

You should say the name of Jesus to all people you meet, on the street, at work, or if you are waiting in a queue of people, move the name of Jesus in your heart and with your lips and turn towards them.

In all, especially among those who upset you and who dislike you, you should adore, worship and serve Jesus. Jesus is imprisoned in many women and men – in their fear and malice, in their sin and misery – free Him by recognizing and worshipping Him in them.

If you walk through the world with this perspective and utter the name of Jesus over every person, the others in front of you will be transformed and transfigured. You will become more and more able to give yourself up to serve people, and for you the word of the gospel will come true in the holy name of Jesus: *"Blessed are they who have a pure heart, for they will see God!"*

7. "Be Lovers of your souls and the souls of your Co-sisters" – cultivating a Culture of the Soul"

Introduction

I gather myself and make myself aware: During the first week of the school of prayer – based on the experience of St. Clare – the importance of the soul and its relationship to the spiritual life were addressed. How strongly and with which emotions do I remember that impulse? Did it resonate with me? What developed within me and in which way?

1. St. Clare and the soul

In the spiritual teachings of St. Clare, the topic of the "soul" has a significant place. In the blessing she left behind to present and future sisters, she specially emphasizes: *"You should always be in love for God, for your own soul and for the soul of your sisters..."* The occurrences while she was dying indicate that she led an intense soul life during that time. A fellow sister witnesses how she speaks to her soul and encourages it: *"Go without anxiety,"* she said, *"for you have a good escort for your journey. Go,"* she said, *"for He Who created you has made you holy. And, always protecting you as a mother her child, He has loved you with a tender love. May you be blessed, O Lord,"* she said, *"You Who have created my soul!"* (LegCl 46:19-22). These words make it clear that she is doing something that she has practised all her life: dialogue with her soul.

2. What is "the soul"?

- In the writings of the men and women who have
  encountered God, a mysterious ability is always
  mentioned, an ability which awakened in them
  and connected them to God. They tell us
  analogously: It was neither my physical senses
  that came into play, nor my feelings, nor my
  intelligence, but a "purpose" in me, which I was
  not aware of until then.

- Psychological treatises do not deal with what we
  are talking about. Even the men and women who
  have experienced it do not know what to call it.
  They use different terms: *"primal ground"*, *"peak
  of the soul"* (St. Augustine), *"mind"* (Tauler),
  "spirit of the soul" (St. Teresa of Avila), *"middle
  of the soul"* (St. John of the Cross), *"the fine tip
  of the soul"* (St. Johanna von Chantal). These
  saintly people all needed a new term to express
  this new experience. They knew that this
  "spiritual" sense was in them, but at the same time
  was bound, hidden and withered. Only contact
  with God brought it back to life.

- What can we say theologically about the soul? The
  soul is a center of life that moves, affects and
  shapes our bodies and our history. Apparently,
  there is a draft of our life in the soul that has an
  urge to take shape (form). The soul strives to make
  man what he is designed for. So, we are a soul-
  body unit, in which both areas are related. The
  soul prepares its body and works through the body
  in the world.
  The soul, in turn, has a core, a center, or depths
  from which its activity originates. There is
  evidently "the place" where man can live in close
  connection with God; He Himself as the origin of

my existence is present. Mechthild of Magdeburg (1207–1282) says:

"God speaks to the soul: Lady Soul, you are so much created into me that between me and you *can be nothing else."*

3. Spiritual life needs a "culture of the soul"

In the language of the Bible, the soul is also called "heart". The fall of man corrupted the heart of man, so that the spiritual senses became dull, meaning we can no longer directly relate to God. We are "outside", looking for Him in a way that remains useless and only leads to disappointment.

Spiritual life, from this perspective, means regaining soul life. St. Clare says that the body must be *"placed under the law of your soul"*. She knows profoundly: Only if you love your soul, can you find Christ in you and consent wholeheartedly to His redeeming work: For *"only the believing soul is His abode and His (throne) seat"* (3LAg 22). It takes the loving approval of this destiny to be created towards Him, to carry Him within oneself. But this can only be given to me by the soul in freedom and in the Holy Spirit.

Against the programs of negation and suppression of the soul in today's world, a *"culture of the soul"* is needed, which encompasses various areas:

- The awakening of the soul *(God's deeds in me, which I must interpret as such)*

- Living from the soul *(a decision against the tendency to want to be strong and autonomous out of "my Ego")*

- Knowing your soul *(the return to our inwardness)*

- Loving your soul *(loving the simplicity and poverty of the soul)*

- Nourishing your soul *(food can be: God's word and Sacrament, nature, music, poetry, writing, ...)*

- Listening to your soul *(learning the language of symbols, perceiving "touches" in the outer world, dreams)*

- Trusting your soul *(trusting the intuition to be led into inner obedience, against our one-sided ratio)*

- To rejoice about your soul *(joy through the experience of the indwelling of God in the soul)*

4. Exercise

As the exercise for this week, I recommend seeking the *"conversation with my soul"*. This can be done by

A) Addressing my soul directly with the following prayer:

O soul, you most beautiful of all creatures,
how much do you long
to know the place where your lover lives
to find Him
and to become one with Him.
You yourself are the place where He dwells
the hiding place where He hides!
Rejoice that your sweetheart
and your hope
are so close to you
and live inside you.
You cannot be without Him at all.
(St. John of the Cross)

B) Acting according to the following instructions:

- ➢ Good sitting position, perceiving your breath, letting it flow
- ➢ Perceiving the body: I am here!

- ➢ I become aware of the gaze of God/Jesus and let myself be gazed upon

- ➢ God/Jesus looks at my soul with love

- ➢ Is there a "glow" in my body? Put your hand where you sense it

- ➢ Looking with God/Jesus at my soul, becoming aware of the longing God/Jesus has to live in me.

- ➢ I relate to my soul with the help of verses from the Psalms:
  "Wake up, my soul!" (Ps 57:9)
  "My soul consumes in yearning for the temple of the Lord. My heart and body rejoice to Him, to Him, the living God." (Ps 84:3)
  "Gladden the soul of your servant, for to you,
  O Lord, do I lift up my soul." (Ps 86:4)
  "As the deer craves fresh water, so does my soul, God, crave for You..." "My soul thirsts for God, for the living God. When shall I come and appear before God?" (Ps 42:2)
  "Why are you cast down, O my soul, and why are you in turmoil within me? Hope in God; for I shall again praise him, my salvation and my God." (Ps 42:11)
  (This is a selection – decision by intuition!)

➢ Repeat a psalm verse and gradually enter into a dialogue with the soul.

➢ Perceive and enjoy the encounter deeply.

➢ Finally, thank God for this grace; when moving on, try to "keep in touch with this depth".

8. The Lord's Prayer – The standard prayer of the minor brothers

Introduction

The Lord's Prayer is the basic prayer of Christianity. We often pray it and feel that we always need to "refill" and deepen it. Which supplications are currently especially alive in me?

1. The Lord's Prayer in the Franciscan origins

Francis strongly recommended the Lord's Prayer to his brothers and to all faithful (see 2LtF21; 1C 45). Perhaps his fondness for this prayer can be explained by the fact that it provided him with the "key word" when dealing with his father. When he gave up his inheritance in public, he explained to the bishop and the people, who listened in surprise: *"Listen to me, all of you, and understand. Until now I have called Pietro di Bernardone my father. But, because I have proposed to serve God, I return to him the money on account of which he was so upset, and also all the clothing which is his, wanting to say from now on: 'Our Father who are in heaven', and not 'My father, Pietro di Bernardone'"* (3C 20).

Reflecting on the words of Jesus and connecting them to what he heard and experienced, he came to deep insights. In addition to the words that he adopted from contemporary models, he came to very original formulations, which are rooted in his personal experience of God and his biography. While church fathers (e.g. Cyprian) wrote long comments on the Lord's Prayer, Francis remains faithful to the atmosphere and form of the Lord's prayer by extending the salutation at the beginning and then each of the seven petitions. As an interpretation, however, his explanation of the Lord's Prayer is not just a prayer text, but above all instruction and preaching.

2. Meditation of St. Francis inspired by the Lord's Prayer (PrOF)

¹O our Father most holy: Our Creator, Redeemer, Consoler and Savior;
²Who are in heaven: In the angels and the saints, enlightening them to know, for You, Lord, are light; inflaming them to love, for You, Lord, are love; dwelling in them and filling them with happiness, for You, Lord, are Supreme Goodness, the Eternal Good, from Whom all good comes, without Whom there is no good.
³Hallowed be Your Name: May knowledge of You become clearer in us so that we may know the breadth of Your blessings, the length of Your promises, the height of Your majesty, the depth of Your judgements (see Eph 3:18).
⁴Your kingdom come: That You may rule in us through Your grace and enable us to come to Your kingdom where there is a clear vision of You, perfect love of You, blessed companionship with You, eternal enjoyment of You.
⁵Your will be done on earth as in heaven: That we may love You with our whole heart by always thinking of You, with our whole soul, by always desiring You, with our whole mind by always directing all our intentions to You, and by seeking Your glory in everything, with all our whole strength by exerting all our energies and affections of body and soul in the service of Your love and of nothing else; and we may love our neighbor as ourselves by drawing them all to Your love with our whole strength, by rejoicing in the good of others as in our own, by suffering with others at their misfortunes, and by giving offense to no one (see 2 Cor 6,3).
*⁶Our daily bread: Your own beloved Son, our Lord Jesus Christ, **give us this day**: in remembrance, understanding, and reverence of that love which [our Lord Jesus Christ] had for us and of those things that He said and did and suffered for us.*
⁷Forgive us our trespasses: through Your ineffable mercy, through the power of the passion of Your beloved Son and

through the merits and intercession of the ever-blessed Virgin and all Your chosen.

⁸As we forgive those who trespass against us: *And what we do not completely forgive, Lord make us forgive completely that we may truly love our enemies because of You and we may fervently intercede for them before You, returning no one evil for evil and we may strife to help everyone in You (see 1 Thess 5:15; Rom 12:17).*

⁹And lead us not into temptation: *hidden or obvious, sudden or persistent.*

¹⁰But deliver us from evil: *past, present and future.*

3. A step further

- Francis begins the prayer with *"O Our Father Most Holy"* (1st verse). Both words preceding "Father" are typical for Francis: The invocative "O" is also found in the amazed expression of joy in the Letter to the Faithful, while "Most Holy" as an attribute to "Father" often appears in the Office of the Passion.

  In the extended salutation we again find references to the great veneration of St. Francis for the Most Holy Trinity: *"our Creator, Redeemer, Consoler and Savior"* means Father (= Creator), Son (= Redeemer) and Holy Spirit (= Consoler).

  Mentioning the Son twice (Redeemer = Jesus Christ as "Son of Man", "Savior" means the returning Lord) gives the Trinitarian formula a christological aspect. Together with the little doxology at the end of the Lord's Prayer declaration, the Trinitarian framework is formed.

- In the continuation of the salutation *"Who are in heaven: In the Angels and in the Saints"* (2nd verse) reflects the belief in the inseparable community between itinerant and glorified church. "Heaven" is not fixed as a place but is seen in persons: "You dwell in them." A person's heart becomes heaven, in so far as he opens himself to the call to holiness and participates in God Himself.

- That is why from the third verse on, the Lord's prayer is about ourselves: in us the realization of God shall shine forth, in us his reign should begin. As God is in the Saints, he should be in us more and more until we come to the undisguised view of God himself. Heaven and earth, saints and sinners embrace the bond of close communion. In asking for forgiveness of our guilt, we can rely on *"the merits and intercession of the ever-blessed Virgin and all Your elect."* as verse 7 says. For Francis *"the itinerant church of sinners is inseparably united with the perfect church of saints. Ultimately, it is this believing, broad view of the church that carries him over the shortcomings and weaknesses of the church and makes him irrevocably stand by her"* (Leonhard Lehmann, "Tiefe und Weite", p. 170).

- In contrast to the prevailing ecclesiastical views, Francis does not interpret the "kingdom of God" politically in the fourth verse; he does not even refer to the Church, but understands it to be a transcendental dimension: the relationship of man to God. *"The Kingdom of God is a possibility, an opportunity; by grace it is initially in us, it is finally revealed as a communion with God"* (Leonhard Lehmann, "Tiefe und Weite", p. 169). The length of the 5th verse alone shows that a central theme for Francis is being developed here, the theme of total dedication to God, radical and boundless love. The verse offers us an interpretation of the main commandment of Jesus, which is combined with the Lord's Prayer *"Your will be done!"*. In this way, Francis makes it clear that God's will is love! God's will happens *in heaven* when we love *him*: God's will happens *on earth* when we love *each other*. For love of God and neighbor, concrete examples and behaviors are then named, which are determined by radicalism and universality (the words "always", "completely", "all", "in everything", "nothing else", "nobody"!).

- The theme of charity is continued in the 8th verse, which deals with complete forgiveness. The three adverbs *"forgive completely", "truly love", "I fervently intercede"* and the contrast between *"no one – all"* urge willingness for universal reconciliation. Nobody should be excluded from our love, not even enemies. The deed of God continues in the act of the believer. That we should love one another is not a moral demand, but a concrete answer to God's love for us, who first loved us and revealed the meaningfulness of boundless love to us.

- Hence, the plea for daily bread in verse six is interpreted in a Eucharistic manner: the love of the Triune God gives itself anew every day in the gift of the Eucharist, it gives itself humbly into the hands of the believer. In the total devotion of the Incarnate Son, this limitless love has been revealed, which remains permanently present in the form of the Eucharist.

4. Exercise

For this week's exercise I recommend the contemplation of the meditation on the Lord's Prayer in sections according to the "Franciscan Three-Steps" of con-templation (see introduction).

Day 1	Salutation *(with rumination = repetitions and own invocations)*
Day 2	Verse 2+3
Day 3	Verse 4
Day 4	Verse 5
Day 5	Verse 6+7
Day 6	Verse 8
Day 7	Verse 9+10

(The impulses are taken from the book by Leonhard Lehmann OFMCap, Tiefe und Weite. Der universale Grundzug in den Gebeten des Franziskus von Assisi (Franziskanische Forschungen Heft 29), Werl 1984.)

9. The "Praise of God at La Verna" as a commitment to the fullness of God and the creaturely poverty of man

Introduction

I gather myself and, with loving attention, perceive my prayer experiences in the previous practices of the "Franciscan School of Prayer".
Where did my wanting and "doing" reach a limit? Do I feel pressure to "improve" myself through more performance? Or did I recognize more of my poverty in prayer and also begin to accept it with inner affirmation?

1. Francis and his love of poverty

When we talk about poverty, we usually do so with a negative connotation, even if we mean voluntary poverty. Poverty appears to us in the guise of renunciation, but not so to St. Francis and his brothers, for whom poverty is wealth.
They even believe that it characterizes the original situation of man and belongs to existence in paradise. That is what man has to return to. In a scripture, the "Sacrum Commercium", poverty itself says to Francis: *"A long, long time ago I was in the paradise of my God (Rev 2:7), where man was naked. Yes, I walked in the man and with the naked man through that whole glorious garden, without fear and hesitation, without suspicion of anything hostile. And I thought I was with him forever; for the very Most High created him right, good, and wise, and placed him in the loveliest and most beautiful place. My joy was exceedingly great, and I always played before him (Prov. 8:30); as he had nothing on possession, he belonged to God"* (ScEx 8:1-2).

According to these words, poverty is the dignity of man, his direct access to God: nothing stands between him and God; the less he has, the more he is God's. Poverty is just another word for "being the creature of God", "belonging to God".

The confession of poverty is therefore a confession to God the Creator, who creates all that is good, beautiful, true, who gives all being life. Poverty, thus, wants to explore the idea of being a creature in all its profundity: everything, the whole, should belong to God and only should be given to man in the manner of a gift, for which the Creator is to be thanked always and at all times.

2. Francis in the tension of creaturely poverty and divine fullness

Prayer was the preferred place for Francis to meet his own existential poverty and to be gifted with the overwhelming fullness of God. Growing in the immediacy to God confronted him more and more with the reality of his own soul, which is "a nothing" in itself, pure receiving and passing on of life that does not come from it.

Isn't abject poverty the state that most corresponds to our human soul and by which we are most true in our being? The whole wealth of God could pour itself into His soul and make Francis truly joyful.

A witness of this existential prayer experience is also St. Theresa of the Child Jesus (1873–1897), who tells us:

> *"If you are nothing,*
> *You must not forget*
> *that Jesus is everything.*
> *That is why you have to sink*
> *your little nothing*
> *in His*
> *infinite everything*
> *and you are only allowed to*

think of this
only lovable everything."

In addition to the "Blessing Prayer", the "The Praises of God" is the Franciscan witness to this experience of poverty in form of prayer.

3. "The Praises of God"

"You are the holy, Lord God, who does wonderful things.
You are strong.
You are great.
You are the most high.
You are the almighty king, You, holy Father,
King of heaven and earth.
You are three and one;
The Lord God of gods,
You are the good, all good, the highest good,
Lord God living and true.
You are love and charity.
You are wisdom.
You are humility.
You are patience.
You are beauty.
You are meekness.
You are security.
You are rest.
You are gladness and joy.
You are our hope.
You are justice.
You are moderation.
You are all our riches to sufficiency.
You are beauty.
You are meekness.
You are the protector.
You are our custodian and defender.
You are strength.

You are refreshment.
You are our hope.
You are our faith.
You are our charity.
You are all our sweetness.
You are our eternal life.
Great and wonderful Lord, Almighty God, Merciful Savior."

4. Exercise

This week we shall be focusing on the "The Praises of God". This text can only be meditated with great care, after a long, deep silence and listening to yourself. Slowly, as when large drops of water fall at longer intervals, you form the individual calls internally.

> ➢ I gather myself in the presence of God and find peace.

> ➢ I begin to praise and repeat the individual invocations slowly (as described above).

> ➢ I let myself be drawn into great silence if it pleases God.

10. "Perfect Joy"

Introduction

I perceive my inner longing for deep, genuine joy.

1. Francis is determined by paschal joy

Easter is the beginning of a deeper joy in the world. By transcending the cross, a whole new joy enters into the world, a complete joy. Easter joy is a joy that can no longer be destroyed by problems and difficulties, but which is so deep that it is a perfect joy in the midst of difficulties.

An overwhelming joy often burst forth despite the many sufferings and weaknesses that beset St. Francis. That is why he was able to write the Canticle of the Sun or 'play the violin' with two wooden sticks. He always reminds his brothers to be happy and cheerful in their faith. *"Let them be careful not to appear outwardly as sad and gloomy hypocrites but show themselves joyful, cheerful and consistently gracious in the Lord"* (ER 7:16).

However, this complete joy is not a superficial joy, but a deep, purified joy that has gone through many problems and doubts. The story of "Perfect Joy" is therefore a typical Franciscan story.

2. The tale of perfect joy

As Saint Francis was once walking with Brother Leo from Perugia to Saint Mary of the Angels in wintertime, and the very great cold stung him sharply, he called Brother Leo, who was walking in front and said this to him:

[1] *"Brother Leo, if it should happen that the Lesser brothers in every land should be a great example of holiness and give good edification, nonetheless write and note carefully*

that this is not perfect Joy." And walking along further, Saint Francis called on him a second time:

[2] "O Brother Leo, even if a Lesser Brother gives sight to the blind, straightens the limbs of the crippled, drives out an attack of demons, restores hearing to the deaf and walking to the lame, speech to the mute and, what is even greater, raises those who have been dead for four days, write that this is not perfect joy." And walking on a little, Saint Francis cried out loudly:

[3] "O Brother Leo, if a lesser brother knew all languages, all the sciences and all the Scriptures, if he knew how to prophesy and reveal, not only future things, but also the secrets of the conscience and of every man, write that this is not perfect joy." Walking on a bit further, Saint Francis cried out even louder:

[4] "O Brother Leo, little lamb of God, even though a Lesser Brother may speak with the tongue of an angel and knows the course of the stars and the powers of herbs, and all the treasures of the earth were revealed to him, and he knew the virtues of birds, fish and all animals and stones and waters, write that this is not perfect joy." And walking along a bit, Saint Francis cried out loudly:

[5] "O Brother Leo, even if a Lesser Brother knew how to preach so well that he converts all the unbelievers to the faith of Christ, write that this is not perfect joy."

[6] After they had been talking for a good two miles, Brother Leo with great amazement asked him and said: "Father, I ask you, for the sake of God, tell me what perfect joy is."

[7] And Saint Francis replied to him: "When we come to Saint Mary of the Angels, soaked from rain like this and frozen from the cold and covered with mud and suffering from hunger, and we knock at the door, and the porter comes out angrily and says, 'Who are you?' and we say: 'We are two of your brothers', and he says: 'You're not telling the truth: you two are scoundrels who go around tricking people and stealing the alms of the poor. Go away,' and he doesn't open for us, and makes us stay outside in the snow and rain, cold and hungry until night-time, then we patiently endure such insults and cruelty and

abuse without becoming upset or complaining about him, and think humbly that that porter in fact recognizes us, that it is God who makes him speak against us: O Brother Leo, write that this is perfect joy.

[8] *And if we even continue knocking and he comes out angrily, and drives us away with curses and blows, like annoying vagrants, saying: 'Get out of here, you dirty little thieves, go to the hospital, because you're not going to eat here or stay here'; if we endure this patiently and with happiness and love, O Brother Leo, write that this is perfect joy.*

[9] *And if, driven by hunger and cold and darkness we knock even more and call out and beg for the love of God with loud crying so that he opens the door for us and lets us at least come inside, and he becomes angrier and says: 'These are annoying vagrants, I'll pay them well for what they're worth', and comes outside with a knobbly stick and grabs us by the hood and throws us on the ground and rolls us in the snow and beats us from head to toe with that stick; if we endure these things patiently and with happiness, thinking of the sufferings of the blessed Christ, which we must endure for His love, O Brother Leo, write that here and in this is perfect joy" (Fioretti 8).*

3. Suggestions for understanding the tale

This story is not a story about un-Christian masochism that wants to endure suffering for the sake of suffering. The point of the narrative lies in the patience and cheerfulness that, despite the suffering and contempt, is in Francis' heart – yes, it is precisely in the suffering. Real joy does not lie in personal or professional success, in the success of the community or family, or in the success of the church, but in being anchored deep in Jesus and in the intimate relationship with Him. This alone prevents agitation and gives patience and serenity in the midst of failure and depression.

Perfect joy lies in the fact that I can discover that my roots in Christ are so deep that I am no longer dependent on success or failure, but that I can stand very deeply rooted in God, in good and bad days. I know I am carried and held by God in the dark. This belief grows in distress and with great patience.

(Bibliography for *"Perfect Joy"*: Lothar Hardick, *Die wahre und vollkommene Freude des heiligen Franziskus*, Werl, 1981.)

4. Exercise

First read the text as a whole and then again in sections over the course of the week. Choose a part of the text freely and consider an element of the narrative from a situation in your own life.

> ➤ Have I ever experienced such perfect or even imperfect joy in the midst of failure and difficult situations? Where and when? What can I learn it for the future?

> ➤ Which concrete life situation(s) does the tale present to my inner eye? Is there a hidden longing for God that I want to become aware of?

> ➤ Proceed in the "Three Steps of Franciscan Contemplation" as in the Contemplation of God's Word (see introduction).

11. The Prayer of Obedience

Introduction

I gather myself and experience the powerlessness I am exposed to in my life: in relationships, in teams and committees, etc. I do not let myself be drawn into a mood of resignation but relativize myself by laying all experiences in God's Hands. I acknowledge His "ultimate" responsibility for my life.

1. The historical background of the prayer

The prayer marks the end of the "Letter to the entire Order" (LtOrd) which Francis wrote after his return from the Orient. He met Pope Honorius III in February or March 1220 in Viterbo and made the Pope's concerns his own by passing them on to the friars of his order, to the superiors, the priests and to all the brethren.
Between the lines, there is some bitter disappointment about his own brotherhood, for example when talking about brothers who do not follow the rule of discipline or vagabonding brothers. In his long absence, dissolution grew among the brothers, and divisive tendencies had spread, endangering his original ideals. A turbulent struggle for the appropriate rule and its interpretation was in progress.
In this affliction, he prays together with the brothers for the loving obedience of Jesus Christ.

2. The text of the prayer

"Almighty, eternal, just and merciful God, give us miserable ones
the grace to do for You alone
what we know you want us to do

and always to desire what pleases You.
Inwardly cleansed,
inwardly enlightened and
inflamed by the fire of the Holy Spirit,
may we be able to follow in the footsteps of Your beloved
Son, our Lord Jesus Christ, and,
by Your grace alone,
may we make our way to You, Most High,
Who live and rule in perfect Trinity
and simple Unity,
and are glorified
God almighty, forever and ever.
Amen. " (LtOrd 50-52)

3. Suggestions for understanding the prayer

In this prayer Francis gives a short version of the contemplative path.

Step 1: Looking at God

Almighty, eternal, just, and merciful God …
Francis approaches God with a long salutation in which he assigns four attributes to him. God is *Almighty*: everything is in his power, without him we can do nothing, we stand in his grace alone.
God is the *Eternal*: He has no beginning and end and encompasses the whole of time.
God is the *Just*: Francis knows about the impending last judgement and therefore always reminds us in his letters to live in such a way that one can face the judgement of God.
But God is also the *Merciful*: He does not stop at His position as judge, but he does not portray him one-sidedly either by describing him as just judging or just being soft.

Step 2: Recognize oneself in the face of God's love

... *give to us miserable ones* ...
Now the gaze of St. Francis focuses on man. Given the
greatness, power and love of God, Francis recognizes his
wretchedness, his fragility, his brokenness and sinfulness.

Step 3: Search for the will of God and the answer of love

**... *for You alone what we know you want us to do and
always to desire what pleases You* ...**
The longing to adapt to the will of God is a central issue
for Francis. He therefore emphasizes "wanting" twice.
First, we should do what we know God wants, and second,
we should always want what God wants, which means we
must also accept God's will internally. The total focus on
God, as the center of willing and doing, is the basic
concern of St. Francis.
The extent to which Francis is concerned with this request
for unselfish intent, for the purity of the heart, is shown by
the addition: *"for You alone"*. The purity of heart is the
original state of man before the Fall. Man was made clear
and pure by God, real and honest. Achieving purity of
heart is therefore a return to the original relationship with
God. The earthly and the external no longer block our view
of God. The world becomes transparent towards God
again. Longing for the heavenly begins to shape people
again. Man begins to seek the reality of God again.

Step 4: To follow in the footsteps of Jesus

**... *Inwardly cleansed, inwardly enlightened and
inflamed by the fire of the Holy Spirit, may we be able to
follow in the footprints of Your beloved Son, our Lord
Jesus Christ* ...**
Now the way is described by which we can – being fully
attentive to the will of God – reach God.
The will of God is that we follow in the *footsteps* of His
beloved Son. Just as he obeyed the will of the father

throughout his life, through suffering and death, so we too should do the will of the father by following the Son. In the steps, Francis lists the three classic ways to be unified with God, which Bonaventura then unfolds in his writings:

1. *The path of purification* is followed by the *meditatio*, the contemplative way of reading. Here, the conscience should be sharpened so that man can live in the constant approach to God = life in penitence.

2. *The path of enlightenment* is followed by the practice of *prayer*. The more pure-heartedly we look at God, the more we are enlightened by God and filled with virtues.

3. *The path of mystical union or transformation*, which one can approach through observation or *contemplation*, but can never be reached by oneself. When you are on the way to the Father with the Son and the Holy Spirit, the spirit of love between Son and Father, is present in this dynamic. It is the inner glow which should ignite us and through which we should be drawn ever deeper into this love:
   o In the constant purification of our thoughts and senses,
   o in desisting from self-will against God,
   o in the constant turning to the light of God and in a burning desire for God, nourished and kept alive by the Holy Spirit, we follow in the footsteps of Jesus. Thus, God stands at the beginning and the end of prayer and is the way itself in Jesus Christ.

Step 5: Triune life

... and, by Your grace alone, may we make our way to You, Most High, Who live and rule in perfect Trinity and simple Unity, and are glorified God almighty, forever and ever. Amen.

In the end, Francis sees once again what man does and wants and also the work of God's grace: man must want and do what God pleases, yet it is God alone who saves by grace and gives us communion with Himself.

This god transcends all our ideas of space and time. He rules through all the ages. In the end, sovereignty, greatness, glory and eternity come back into the focus of prayer. If we accept the gift of grace, we have a share in them, do not suffocate the fire of the spirit, turn to the light and remain faithful to the path of the life of Jesus. By leading a Eucharistic life, we are already participating in the Triune Life.

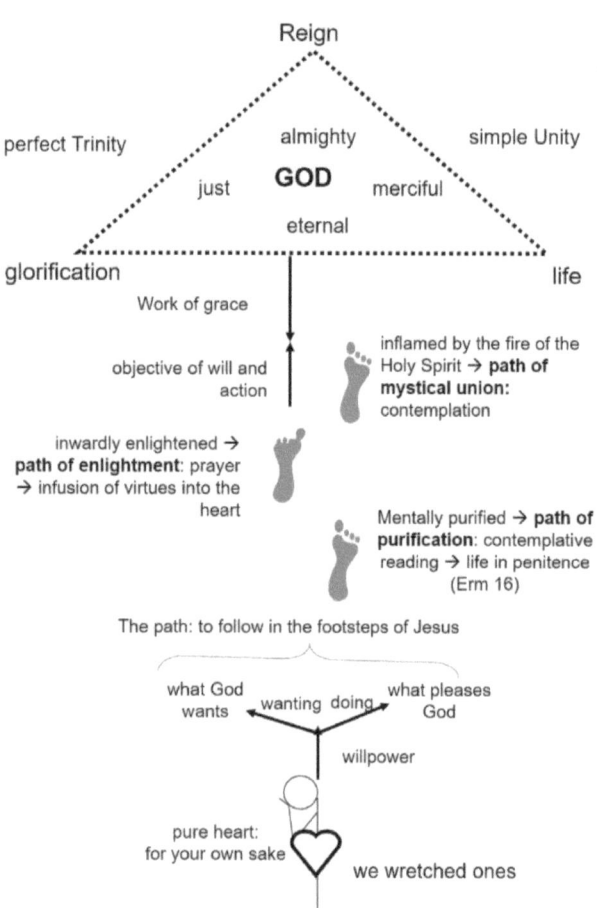

The path: to follow in the footsteps of Jesus

4. Exercise

> ➤ I perceive my state of prayer and stand in the presence of God. I get in touch with Francis and step with him before God: "Teach me to pray, you who have preceded me in the life of following Jesus!"

➤ I ruminate the prayer of obedience in the rhythm of breathing. I allow concrete situations from my life to arise in my consciousness. I request the willingness to join Francis in the movement of prayer in relation to the situations I have contemplated.

➤ I let go of my thinking, wanting, judging and feeling, and I am ready to be transformed by the Triune God in the sense of the prayer that *"by Your grace alone, may we make our way to You."*

12. To follow the patient God in patience

Introduction

Francis repeatedly calls God the *"humble and patient God"*. For him, God's patience with man is one of God's most incredible qualities.

With the perseverance of the past millennia, God has offered man his love again and again and with persistent stubbornness, man has repeatedly rejected God's love. "You still haven't understood!" Only very rarely does Jesus sigh because of his apostles (cf. Mt 15:16; 16:9). As human beings we can understand this all the better. And yet Jesus continues to explain patiently and gives himself to those who reject him again and again. That is why we also call God's patience with human beings his loyalty.

Following the patient Lord, we too can grow in patience, indeed, this growth in patience is something very central. Francis had to learn patience with himself and with his brothers, facing many difficulties. Here is how he helps us to see where we are where patience is concerned:

"If all goes his way, the servant of God cannot recognize how great patience and humility are which he holds in himself. But there comes a time when those who must act according to his wishes do the opposite to him: What he has got in terms of patience and humility, is what he holds and nothing more" (Adm 13).

Exercise

> Deepen individual parts of admonition 13 through inner repetition (ruminatio) and try to let the sentences work in you quietly.

> Where are your wishes fulfilled and where not?

> In which areas of life are you currently patient, in which impatient?

> Check whether your opinion on these points is really factual, or whether it is primarily personal (or even selfish)? Try to make a fine distinction between factual and personal.

> Can I remain calm and accept with patience and humility things that would be better if they were different, or will I lose all patience because I feel hurt, ignored, deceived, forgotten ...?

> After reflecting on these questions, keep returning to Francis' phrases and consider them again in your heart.

13. The Path of Purification

Introduction

I read the story below, "Do you know what a pure heart is?" by Leclerc and ask: How does Francis guide Brother Leo to change his perspective?
I ask to be able to look at the path of my own purification from this point of view.

Do you know what a pure heart is?

"Our sister, the spring", cried Francis as he stepped to the creek, "your clarity is a praise of the innocence of the Lord."
"Our sister, the spring", cried Francis as he stepped to the brook, "your clarity is a hymn of praise for the innocence of the Lord." Leo quickly jumped from stone to stone across the stream. Francis followed him a little more slowly. Leo was already on the other bank waiting for him. He watched the clear water splashing across the golden-red sand between the gray stone blocks. When Francis was with him, Leo paused for a while. Apparently he couldn't tear himself away from this spectacle. Francis looked at him. Leo looked sad. "You are pondering, it seems to me."
"Yes, if we had been granted a bit of this purity, then we would also have had the foolish, exuberant joy of our sister spring and the irresistible power of her water." He stared melancholically at the brook - an image of purity that is out of man's reach forever.
"Come on", said Francis, pulling him with him. The two set off again. They were silent for a while, then Francis asked: "Do you know, brother, what a pure heart is?"
"If you have nothing to blame yourself for", replied Leo without thinking twice.
"Then I understand that you are sad, something you always have to reproach yourself with."

"Exactly, and that is why I gave up hope for a pure heart."
"Oh, brother Leo, don't worry so much about the purity of heart! Look at God! Admire him! Rejoice that He exists, Him, the Very Saintly being! Give thanks to Him for His Own sake. That, my little brother, means having a pure heart. And if you have turned to God, above all, never turn back on yourself! Do not ask yourself how you stand with God! The grief that you are not perfect and that you discover the sinner within yourself is a still human, too human feeling. You have to look higher, much higher. There is God, there is God's infinity and His immutable glory. A heart is pure if it does not stop worshipping the living and true Lord. It takes a deep part in God's life and is so strong that in all its misery it can still be touched by eternal innocence and joy. Such a heart is both empty and full to the brim. That God is God is enough for it. From this certainty it draws all its peace and joy. And the holiness of a heart, is also nothing other than God."

"But God demands that we make an effort and remain faithful", Brother Leo objected.

"Certainly, but holiness is not about realizing yourself and not about fulfilling yourself. Holiness is first and foremost emptiness that one finds in oneself, that one accepts and that God fills to the extent that one opens oneself to his fullness."

"Look, our nothingness, if we accept it, becomes an empty space in which God can still act as a creator. The Lord does not allow anyone to contest his glory. He is the Lord, the Unique, the Only Saintly being. But he takes the poor by the hand, pulls them out of their misery and places them among the princes of his people, so that he may see God's glory. God makes himself the heaven above his heart."

"Brother Leo, the highest demand of that love that the Spirit of the Lord continuously instills in our hearts is: to immerse yourself in the glory of God; amazed to discover that God is God for all eternity and is beyond what we are and can be; be wholeheartedly happy that He exists; be enthusiastic about His eternal youth, to thank Him for Himself and for His never failing mercy. That means

having a pure heart. But you cannot achieve this purity by plaguing yourself."

"But how?" Asked Brother Leo.

"Just give up on yourself. By refusing to keep anything. Also, stop closely researching your own misery. Clear the air. Accept your own misery. Shed all your burdens, even the burden of our mistakes. Just keep in mind the glory of the Lord and expose yourself to His radiance. God exists, that is enough. Then the heart becomes light. It no longer feels like the lark floating drunk in the blue of the vast sky. The heart has done with all the worry and unrest. Its desire for perfection has turned into a simple, pure yes to God."

Leo walked in front of Francis and listened thoughtfully. Gradually his heart became lighter, and great peace came over him.

(Shortened version of "One cannot prevent the sun from shining"): Eligius Leclerc, Wisdom of a Poor. One year in the life of Francis of Assisi, Kevelaer, 2011.)

1. Purification happens through the process of prayer

The life-cycle of our prayer is a lifelong cleansing process. By deciding to take part in the "Franciscan School of Prayer", I agree to go deeper into a journey of purification. The fruits of this journey are true self-knowledge, inner peace and the joy in God. Contemplative reading is an aid on this journey.

2. The path of purification according to Bonaventura (De triplici via)

St. Bonaventura sees three dangers of how man can lose God as the inner center of his life:

- our own *carelessness*: God is no longer the center of our lives.
- our own *desires*: God is no longer the focus of our longing.

- our *bad attitude*: We do not want the good anymore.

2.1 Carelessness

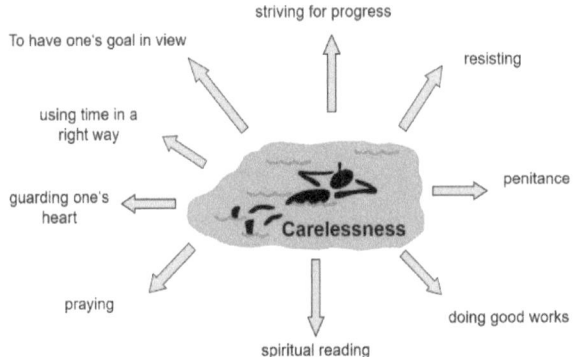

"Carelessness" indicates misdirection through passivity, lethargy, or thoughtless indifference which has become a habit, especially in one's spiritual life. It is important to pay close attention to all these things, so that the heart, well-guarded, uses time profitably and so that the desired goal is considered first in every action. Carelessness can also deprive us of our spiritual progress by preventing us from resisting evil and continually realigning ourselves to God. Finally, it can stop us from seeing that our lives bear good fruit. Bonaventura counteracts negligence with vigor. In a sense, it is a strength of the spirit, which dispels all negligence and enables the soul to carry out all the work of God attentively, full of confidence and with ease. It enables us to deal responsibly and consciously with our own lives.

2.2 Desires

Desire, the instincts themselves, are not bad. They involve an active pursuit of a good that is positive and vital. What is meant here is excessive desire, sacrificing everything good for one's own pleasure. According to Bonaventura, this false, excessive desire encounters man in three forms:

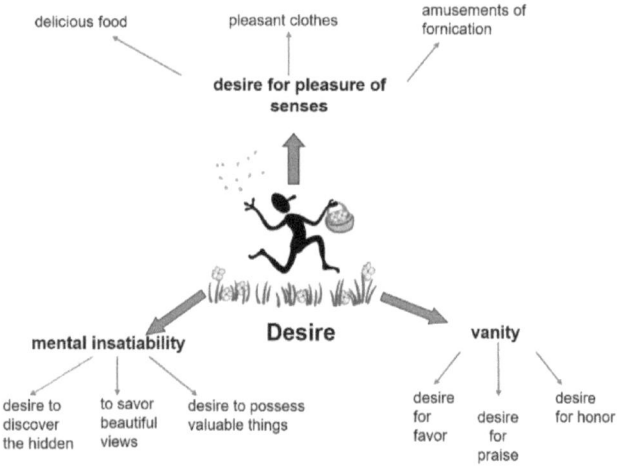

a) in the form of desire for sensual p*leasures*
b) in the form of *spiritual insatiability* and
c) in *vanity*.

- The desire for sensual *pleasure* extends to physically filling my inner emptiness through secondary "forms of nourishment": food or compensatory oral satisfaction. Instead of using my inner emptiness or lack of fulfilment as a motivation to seek God, I stuff myself, so that I no longer have to endure my emptiness.
  Secondly, Bonaventura mentions *physical and sensual softening* and *fornication*. Where I abuse my power of love, which is created for a counterpart, just to give myself pleasure without

really being aware of others, I fall out of the order of love.

- The vice of greed also includes *vanity*. The legitimate desire to be something, to be successful, to be respected, is perverted to pride and arrogance by using all my strength to strive for favor, praise, and honor – whatever the cost.

- In addition to the *greed for valuable and beautiful things*, Bonaventura is also concerned with pure curiosity, with curious talk about others; rummaging in the dirt of others while your own mistakes are overlaid by the faults of others. All these things are connected to spiritual insatiability.

Bonaventura opposes *the sin of desire* with self-discipline and realignment, which also requires a firmness of the spirit that captivates every desire and enables the soul to love a hard, poor and despised life.

2.3 A Bad Attitude

The third root sin is by no means harmless "malice" or "uselessness", but something very serious: the *joy of evil*. Bonaventura sees a bad attitude in *anger*, in *envy* and in *aversion to the good*. These three attitudes make the soul angry.

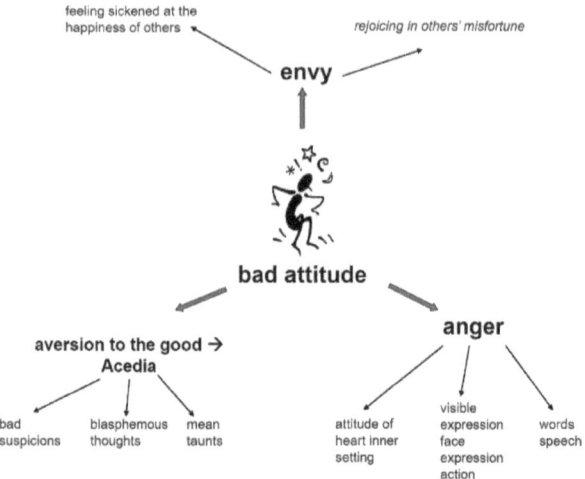

feeling sickened at the happiness of others

rejoicing in others' misfortune

envy

bad attitude

anger

aversion to the good →
Acedia

bad suspicions	blasphemous thoughts	mean taunts

attitude of heart inner setting	visible expression face expression action	words speech

- *Envy* arises not only because you do not have something that the other has – that is, out of desire – but it is rooted in begrudging others' happiness. Therefore, envy goes hand in hand with malicious joy. You can recognize jealousy by the fact that someone becomes completely sick when confronted with someone else's happiness and is happy when the other person is facing misfortune. Since envy cannot even grant one's own talents, which come from the Holy Spirit, Bonaventure counts the sin of envy as a sin against the Holy Spirit.

- *Anger* does not simply mean an anger which may even be righteous, but a passion in which one has a certain joy in being angry with someone and being hostile towards them. It has its place both in the mind as in a visible expression and in the spoken word. It can express itself in the inner attitude as well as in speech or in action. Unforgiveness is cemented in anger.

- A form of bad will hides behind the *aversion to good*. Such a person does not want to be happy about what is good. He can no longer recognize the good sides of his fellow man with joy, but always assumes evil suspicions towards him. There is even the danger that he will no longer be able to enjoy the perfection of God ("blasphemous thoughts").

- Bonaventura mentions goodness and inner joy as a remedy for the evil attitude. These are a "sweetness of the soul" that excludes all evil attitudes and empowers the soul to benevolence, tolerance and inner joy.

3. Exercise

This week we are invited to look at the daily gospels of the third week of Lent, or the current week of the liturgy of the Catholic Church to observe the way Jesus guides people to purification so that they are able to truly love. Look at people, how they get involved or not, what prevents them from following Him. Look into this "mirror" to recognize yourself in it. Jesus Christ also wants to take you on the path of purification. Regarding the individual steps, you can orient yourself by referring to the suggestions of the 1st week of practice (see introduction).
At the end of the time of contemplation, formulate a prayer where you long for this purification.

Examining one's conscience

The following questions can serve as preparation for receiving the Sacrament of Reconciliation in a confession:

- How important is spiritual reading and prayer time in my life? What do I cut out first when my time is short?

- Which influences (pictures, texts, conversations ...) do I expose my heart, my soul to?

- Where are my weak points, which the tempter uses again and again? What about my resistance to these temptations? Do I have a "favorite temptation" that I keep giving in to?

- Do I know situations in which my mind loses control of my desire and my instincts take control of my actions (appetite, desire to buy, gambling, desire to watch TV, sexuality, ...)?

- How do I deal with curiosity if I do not get to know everything I would like to know? Can I let other people keep their secrets?

- How important is it for me to be accepted: by superiors, by people whom I admire? What am I ready to invest?

- How do I deal with failure, slander, and defamation: Can I still stand there in front of myself or do these things pull the ground from under my feet?

- Am I grateful for my life, my life circumstances, or at what points do I struggle with envy?

- How do other people experience my anger or displeasure: through facial expressions, outbursts, offended silence or withdrawal?

- ➤ Are there any people I feel angry about and do not want to forgive? Are there experiences that I use again and again to justify my behavior?

- ➤ Do I practise seeing the good in people, or do I always initially assume that the other is bad?

- ➤ Do I know the secret desire to run down other people?

14. Spiritual Struggles and Difficulties in Praying

Introduction

I gather myself and remember: In what ways have I understood myself more and received encouragement to affirm my spiritual struggle as "normal"?
The following text can help me to deepen my knowledge.

1. Spiritual struggles in one's Prayer-Life

To become able to descend to our own depths and encounter God there, it is important to experience purification. When I look at Christ in contemplation and prayer, I recognize my reality in Him, as in a mirror. I slowly recognize where my body or spirit is at the service of the love of Christ, or if they are guided by other forces. The fight between the power of grace and the power of evil begins. The power of grace seeks to lift everything hidden, crooked, and wounded into the light of Christ, for the power of evil seeks to operate in secret. This spiritual struggle reveals what lies hidden in the heart of man and what his heart itself is: the battlefield on which the drama of the history of salvation takes place, the fight against everything that is spiritually necessary. Since this fight prefers prayer and times of contemplation, it brings considerable prayer difficulties with it.
When we come outwardly into silence, then we first realize that everything inward is anything but quiet. There is a lot of talk in us. It argues or accuses, justifies or calculates, revolts against injustice or failure, compares, massacres and glorifies.

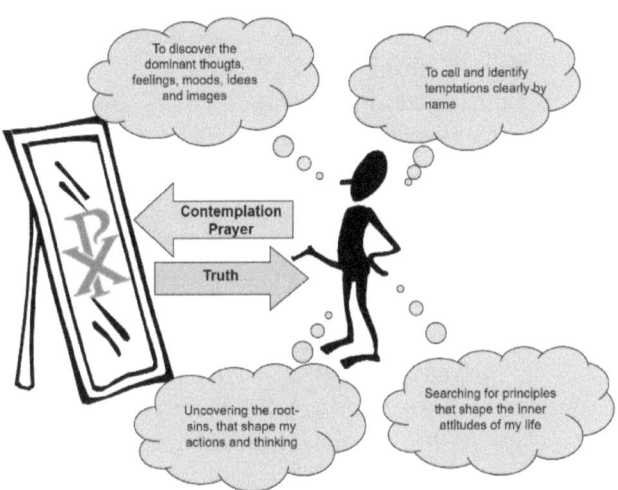

- The desert fathers advise, therefore, first: *to focus attention on one's thoughts*. They do not ask, for example: *What spiritual exercises do you practice? Can you pray well? Do you keep your prayer times? Do you regularly receive the sacraments?* They ask their questions in a different way: *How did you feel when you met your arch enemy today? How was it when the mailbox was empty today or no email came? How did you react when you were not greeted? What did you feel when the food on the table was cold? How do you feel when someone is able or allowed to do what you would like to or could do? Or what images are your favourite temptations?* Thoughts or images expose my true self, and it is often unpleasant to look honestly at your own lives. It is about perceiving where I really am in my life. It is important to lose the illusions about my own life and get a realistic view of it.

- Secondly, the desert fathers advise us *to name* these thoughts *clearly* in a spiritual conversation or in a confessional dialogue and to identify them.

By putting them into words, I can also distance myself from them. What can no longer live undetected in the dark loses much of its effectiveness. I may release my weakness into the weakness of Jesus, who transforms it.

- • Thirdly, the desert fathers advise us to look for the *guiding principles* in which our inner attitudes formulate themselves. Such "script sentences", as we say today, are for example as follows: *"Nobody likes me!", "I cannot do anything!", "I have been forgotten by all of you!", "I am the greatest!", "I am incredibly popular!", "I can never do that!".*

  Such sentences reveal my inner attitude. Since the mind transforms what it deals with, it is important to choose among the various principles the ones that it should deal with. This selection of thoughts which flow through us is, according to the conception of the desert fathers, one of the main tasks of spiritual life; it is supported by the following exercises:
  - frequent spiritual reading,
  - singing of psalms,
  - keeping vigil, fasting, praying

- • And finally, it is necessary to encounter the root sins, which are based on crooked and evil behaving and thinking. The single thoughts conceal vices or root sins, which become effective by provoking certain moods, feelings, ideas and malaise in man.

  More important than the knowledge of single (sinful) instincts, emotions, moods and malaise is the knowledge of their causes, processes and techniques *(→ "How is it that I feel like this right now?", "How is it that I acted that way and not otherwise?")*. It may therefore be helpful to ask about the cause of certain problems, longings, tendencies, and wrong attitudes: *"How did this sin come about?"*, *"Why am I feeling so sad at the moment?"*, *"Why does study/prayer bring me no joy?"*, *"How does it explain that I buy so many things right now?"*...

2. Love grows while overcoming difficulties in prayer

- I should not engage in a conversation with all these *distractions in prayer* during prayer time. I should perceive them and reflect on them after the time of prayer.

- Another difficulty that can arise in prayer is *spiritual dryness*. It is a phenomenon that either indicates a pending purification (something is still blocking one internally), or a threshold in spiritual life at which one is about to reach greater depth. A distinction is only possible through spiritual guidance. In any case, there is a danger in the dryness of falling into *spiritual greed*. Because I no longer find the coveted comfort in my life with God – it no longer tastes good to me – I flee into an abundance of spiritual exercises, literature, spiritual advice, spiritual events etc., instead of standing naked and poor in front of God enduring my poverty.

The vice of *Acedia or carelessness*, which the desert fathers describe as the most dangerous and arduous vice of a spiritually oriented person, will always catch up with us. Evagrius Ponticus described this vice as the noon demon. It causes the sun to stop moving and the makes day have more than 50 hours. It keeps one constantly looking out the window to see if anyone is finally coming to release one from one's boring activity. It injects an aversion to the place where one is and to one's way of life. It causes us to be angry at our brothers/sisters/spouse and be convinced that nobody has comforted us. It makes us long for places and people where we feel better. It pretends that God can be worshipped everywhere and that it does not necessarily have to be here. It awakens the memory of relatives and former life.

According to Bonaventura, Acedia causes man to try to avoid all efforts to participate in his own salvation. It tries to go the easier way. Inner resistance can also go against the spiritual: against prayer time or spiritual reading. I already know that it would be good, but right now I do not want to do it, there are more important things. Acedia expresses itself in carelessness. It can be the gravedigger of any good start.

It may also be that a certain boredom appears (*"I already know what is written there!"*), which can also be paired with fatigue. As soon as I am sitting in my prayer corner, my eyes start to close. Here it is important to distinguish whether the tiredness is real or a temptation. It may even be that there is a kind of aversion inside me that refuses to deliver myself more deeply to God. *The proven weapons against the root sins also apply here: humor, honesty, patience and spiritual guidance.*

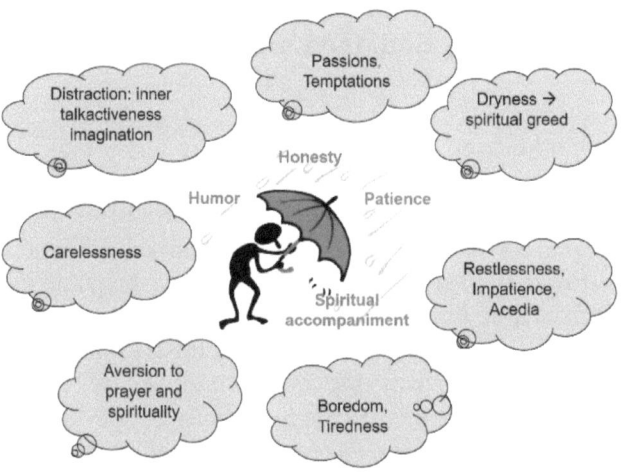

4. Exercise

> This week I continue faithfully in the contemplation of the daily word, which are the texts of the second week of Lent or the current texts of the daily liturgy of the Catholic Church. I stick to the advice for these exercises in the first week of practice.

> I perceive my prayer difficulties, "my battleground", without entangling myself or becoming discouraged. When struggling becomes oppressive, I can use the words of the Letter to the Romans. *"In the same way, the Spirit helps us in our weakness... but the Spirit Himself intercedes for us through wordless groans"* (Rom 8:26), by moving them into the breathing rhythm – or I seek refuge in the Jesus' Prayer.

15. "Consider anything that prevents you from seeking God, the Lord, as grace"

Introduction

Being obviously in great inner turmoil, a superior, a minister of the Franciscan Order, turned to Francis some time between 1218 and 1221 to receive help and guidance from him. Francis wrote him an extraordinary letter, which tries to help the brother in his misery, but which also discreetly reveals the deeper motives of his actions. Francis wrote this "Letter to a Minister" (LtMin) out of the knowledge of his own struggles, out of his own overcome hardship, and described with deep inner peace essential features of life with God and with his brothers and sisters. The letter thus became a fascinating document of a saint who finds serenity in God in the midst of his struggles. Let's look at several sentences and thoughts from this letter. It is good to meditate individual parts of these sentences in one's heart and savour them until their deep truth is unfolded in us.

1. *"I speak to you, as best I can, about the state of your soul. You must consider as grace all that impedes you from loving the Lord God and whoever has become an impediment to you, whether brothers or others, even if they lay hands on you. And may you want it to be this way and not otherwise."*

    You can only swallow several times if you read these sentences. Aren't they completely overwhelming? But Francis writes from his experience. He writes what he has experienced himself. Obstacles and difficulties have taught him the most. Not the nicest, but the most difficult brothers brought him closest to himself and God. That is his life experience.

Everything that I encounter in my life is ultimately grace and an encounter with God – also and especially the obstacles through which I grow. This way I can grow into an inner calmness, into deeper trust in God.

2. *"And love those who do those things to you and do not wish anything different from them, unless it is something the Lord God shall have given you. And love them in this and do not wish that they become better Christians. And let this be of more value than a hermitage for you."*

My desire goes in this or that direction. Sometimes I want something, sometimes the complete opposite of it. For a long time I cannot imagine living without it. And some time later I let it go without even batting an eyelid. I am unsteady and wavering. If I could fix my desire entirely in the will of God, I would have a solid foundation for my life. I could even accept the brothers and sisters with whom I live and work in their uniqueness. I could even drop my hypocritical wishes for others – "I only want the best for them", "I only want to help them so that they can become better Christians". But this is exceedingly difficult to understand, so that some manuscripts of the letter omit the "not" in the second to last sentence. That sounds more familiar: "... you should demand that they are better Christians". On top of that, this uncomfortable conflict situation is "more than a hermitage", into which the troubled minister and Francis would like to withdraw forever (today many people call this "a desert island"). Only those who trust fully in God can become serene and calm.

3. *"And I want to know, if you love the Lord and me, His and your servant, if you do the following, namely: there must not be a brother in the world, even if he has sinned as much as he could sin, who has seen your eyes and then would have to leave you without your mercy, if he seeks mercy."*

The love for God can be recognized by the fact that I am merciful towards my brothers and sisters. That is only natural, I would say. And yet it is so incredibly difficult. Do my eyes really look at others with compassion? Or just from above? Is my gaze a place of mercy for others or a judgement on others? A place to meet God's forgiveness? Do people experience God's gaze in the depth of my gaze?

4. *"And if he does not seek mercy, ask him if he wants mercy. And if he would sin a thousand times before your eyes then, love him more than me, so that you may draw him to the Lord. And with people like this always have mercy."*

To run after people, to ask them if they are not looking for mercy: that is the attitude of Jesus, the Good Shepherd, who is especially concerned about the lost sheep. Our attitude, on the other hand, is often like this: "He, who does not want, has already received." In the attitude of Jesus, Francis once sends a brother after robbers, whom he had harshly rejected when they came begging to a brothers' community. He was told to apologize to them. The robbers, however, abandon their crimes because of the apology of this brother and accept the merciful forgiveness of God (Fioretti 26). Mercy draws men more to the Lord than many clever words.

5. *"Let all the brothers who know that he has sinned not bring shame upon him or slander him; let them, instead, show great mercy to him and keep*

*the sin of their brother very secret because those
who are well do not need a physician, but the sick
do." (Mt 9:12).*

How happily we share the mistakes of others! That
strengthens our self-esteem. The tabloid press
lives from people's mistakes and spread details of
these mistakes. A negative meditation that can
prevent us from doing this is to consider the
Pharisee's sentence in the temple: "Thank you,
God, that I am not like other people, like this tax
collector." We often think of this sentence in
secret. Let us say it occasionally out loud (for
ourselves) so that it is really embarrassing for us.
Which personal name do you want to use for "this
tax collector there"? "Thank you, God, that I am
not ... like this sister there ..., this employee there
..." We sick people need compassion from the
doctor. And he is already there – looking for us ...

6. *"The priests should have no authority (in
confession) to impose a form of repentance other
than this: 'Go and sin no more'" (Jn 8:11).*

Francis completely stands the medieval penitential
system with its costly indulgences (see the
Portiuncula indulgence) on its head. The only
repentance for sin is to stop sinning. God's mercy
is free, given as a gift! Repentance and goodwill
are enough. What is bad, of course, remains bad.
But those who repent and confess may experience
the infinite mercy of God. In confession, the priest
passes on what transcends himself: forgiveness
without limits. Father Leonhard Lehmann
OFMCap calls this "a doctrine of mercy that goes
to extremes". God is extreme. Do I allow myself
to be seduced by God's extreme love?

16. A life of reconciliation

Introduction

The gift of the Risen Lord to His apostles who abandoned and betrayed Him, is forgiveness. He does not consider their failures and their weaknesses, rather He grants them peace. Motivated by the reconciliation they have received, they are sent out into the world to pass it on: *"May peace be with you! I am sending you like the Father has sent me"* (Jn 20:21). He breathes on them, gives them the Holy Spirit and the authority to forgive sins. So, the Risen Lord lives on among them.

Are there any experiences in my life where I was allowed to receive reconciliation as a pure gift of God and it urged me to pass on this forgiving love?

1. Francis becomes the tool of the unity and reconciliation of Christ

The charisma of St. Francis, the innermost gift of grace of his vocation, burst forth in the encounter with the leper and Christ Crucified. It was in this encounter that his heart was touched by the commandment of Jesus: *"Love one another, as I have loved you!"* – this extends from brotherly love to love of the enemy. From the experience of the love of God which ignores all human boundaries, he understood his mission to be a tool of unity and reconciliation among men.

2. How Francis leads his brothers into reconciliation according to the Gospel

In the ninth admonition Francis looks upon Christ on the cross and thus leads us into the center of Christian reconciliation:

"The Lord says, 'Love your enemies. Do good to those who hate you and pray for those who persecute and defame you' (Mt 5:44). Anyway, he who loves his enemy genuinely does not feel pain for the injustice that the other does to himself, but is inflamed because of the sin of his soul for the sake of the love of God. And may he show love to him in actions."

The ninth admonition is not the only passage in the writings of St. Francis where he deals with loving the enemy. It was apparently so very important to him that there is a striking amount of references and explanations of the subject. We can assume that Saint Francis regarded this point as essential for a life in accordance with the Gospels.

We must remember that the aim of Christian love is the love of the enemy. In the love of the enemy there is a force that can change the world. However, for most Christians and religious, this power is an untapped potential. We will only bear fruit in the service of the Kingdom of God, which requires reconciliation and unity, if we are ready and capable of loving our enemies. If we examine our consciences, we can discover enmity towards God (where we feel He is an imposition to us!), enmity towards a human being or a group of people, but also towards ourselves (for example that I reject and repress parts of my personality).

Francis knows about these dimensions when he states in the unconfirmed rule: *"And all the brethren, wherever they are, should remember that they surrendered themselves to the Lord Jesus Christ and left to Him all that was invalid. And for the sake of His love for us, they must expose themselves to the visible as well as the invisible enemies"* (ER 16:10).
He admonishes those who claim to be followers of Jesus, regarding their behavior to the so-called "enemy": "May he show love to him in his actions."

3. The prayer for "the enemy" initiates the process of reconciliation

Prayer should not be confined only to those who sympathize with us, who do good to us and to whom we are committed. It should embrace generously and big-heartedly those who inflict evil on us and defame us. Doing this frees up the dynamic of a reconciliation process for me and the so-called "enemy".

The path of reconciliation is a long one and requires several steps:

- Praying for conversion and reconciliation for me and a person with whom I have a strained relationship.

- Realizing which negative feelings, painful memories, bad inner images and hurtful words I have internalized and cannot forget.

- The willingness to admit negative feelings such as disappointment, hurt, jealousy, anger, but above all the deep pain that goes with it, in order to be able to gradually release them, by handing them over to Jesus Christ, by laying my pain into the pain of Jesus, into his redemptive suffering.

- The willingness to hold an open conversation which will serve reconciliation. This requires renouncing retribution and revenge. God should thereby be a bridge between us.

- The willingness to forgive (myself and the other person) out of awareness that Jesus Christ has obtained forgiveness through His redemptive suffering. It is not "my achievement", but a gift that I want to open up for Him so that He can act inside me. Christ speaks the liberating word: "Father, forgive them, for they do not know what they do" (Luke 23:34).

4. Pain is part of love

In the process of reconciliation, the pain of suffered or committed injustice really comes to light. For the success of reconciliation it is crucial to find a way through the pain. The following text by P. Willi Lambert SJ can help you to deal with pain:

Pain that heals pain
"There are so many things on offer to cure pain: pills, radiation, healing sleep, acupuncture, massages, therapy, drugs, herbal tea, autogenic training... There are hundreds more remedies and ways: all given, advertised, and sold to heal pain.
And here is another one: pain. The pain itself. The pain as a painkiller, pain that heals.
Which pain should this pain primarily heal? Above all, it brings spiritual and mental healing. Anything that makes the soul sick: envy, anger, hate, bitterness, feelings of inferiority, being offended, addiction, disunity, fears, etc...

And what does this 'pain therapy' look like?
Well, it assumes that jealousy, revenge, etc. are not the initial feelings, but are already a first or second reaction to real or feared hurts. Basically, these are feelings we experience to escape something, substitute feelings or prosthetic feelings.
The crucial step of 'pain therapy' is to give the original feeling of pain space. Thus, if someone cuts you off, that hurts! You could let it hurt you, instead of yelling at the other person.
If something does not go according to your wishes, that hurts! You could let it hurt you instead of raging or resigning.
If, if, if ..., 1000 situations, – at the end we can always ask ourselves: Could I not let it hurt a bit now, rather than...

If you again and again get involved in many concrete situations, you will feel a healing success. And that is what it is about. Pain therapy is a biblical form of therapy. Its healing power is guaranteed. At least that is how Jesus sees it. The weeping will laugh! Blessed are those who understand how to suffer pain, for joy will arise in them. God promises us transformation when we bear our pain well. The wounds will be transfigured, as with Jesus. They have healing power, as with Jesus: 'With His wounds we are healed!' writes the prophet Isaiah about the Righteous (Is 53:5). By accepting one's own pain, one can gain access to that healing pain.

There are people who experience this healing power. People who feel that there is not only a succession of pain and joy in their lives, but a simultaneity: in the midst of pain, peace, joy, strength, and hope grow at an even deeper level.

Such pain is not a substitute action or feeling, not a substitute for acting. Such pain 'only' means that we can react more out of peace of heart – or experience the power of suffering if necessary. Pain that heals pain – it exists!"

5. Exercise

As an exercise this week I recommend praying for people who are "enemies" to me and/or to whom I am "an enemy". Here I start from the "three-step Franciscan way of contemplation" (see introduction):

> ➤ I gather myself, also physically, then I catch the gaze of Jesus. I give myself to Him and our relationship.

> ➤ Once I am well anchored in the relationship with Him, I place the "enemy" in front of my inner eye and ask Jesus to look at them with me. I try to look at this person from the perspective of Jesus and gradually try to understand them, their view of

things, their feelings and thoughts. I pay attention to my own feelings towards this person and lay them before Jesus. I am ready to endure pain together with Jesus.

➢ I remain in my request for transformation of my feelings and for mercy for me and my "enemy". I hand myself over to the guidance of God in great confidence and renounce any "desire to be active out of my own impulses".

➢ I repeat the exercise the next day, either with the same person or another person. It is important to pay attention to God's inner guidance and not to avoid the pain that wants to reveal itself.

17. Contemplation of the suffering of Francis and Clare

Introduction

I gather in silence and let experiences arise, where I have experienced transformation in my own or in someone else's suffering. I stay in the memory of how I got through my suffering and became open to the suffering of Jesus.

1. The passionate love of St. Clare for Christ Crucified

St. Agnes of Prague tells Clare about concrete hardship and misery. Clare replies as follows in her fourth letter: *"... Finally contemplate, in the depth of this same mirror, the ineffable charity that He chose to suffer on the tree of the Cross and to die there the most shameful kind of death. Therefore, that Mirror, suspended on the wood of the Cross, warned those passing by that here are things to be considered, saying: 'All you who pass by the way, look and see if there is any suffering like my suffering!' 'Let us respond to Him,' It says, 'crying out and lamenting, in one voice, in one spirit: Remembering this over and over leaves my soul sinking within me!'"* (4 LAg 23-26).

Thus St. Clare urges Agnes of Prague, in her reflections on Christ Crucified to feel with Him, to suffer with Him His abandonment, His grief, to embrace His exceptional love, which is expressed in His suffering. With all her senses, with heart and mind, she enters into a communion of suffering with Christ.

The biography written by Brother Thomas of Celano shows that she was filled with the most ardent love for Christ Crucified. It says: *"She was intimately familiar with the lamentations of the Lord's suffering. To her His sacred wounds were both, a source of bitter feelings and the reason to avoid sweeter pleasures. The tears over the suffering Christ made her quite drunk and she often imagined Him, Whom love had deeply impressed on her heart, in her spirit. She guided her novices to lament about Christ Crucified, and what she taught in words she showed by her own example"* (LegCl 30).

The "Prayer for the Adoration of the Five Holy Wounds" which she prayed regularly has been lost. Only the Office of the Passion, developed by Francis, which she prayed with great love, has been handed down to us.

2. How Francis looks at the suffering of Jesus

In art Francis is often portrayed as finding his place at the wounds of Jesus. The traditional picture leads me to this place in my contemplation.

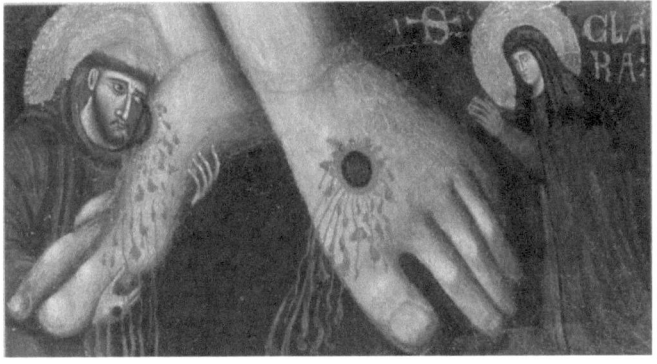

Detail from the altar-cross-icon in Sta. Chiara, Assisi

Francis experienced much inner and outer suffering in his life. However, he did not focus on himself, but looked at his crucified Lord. In his Suffering Psalms, he linked his own sufferings to the sufferings of Jesus and practically followed Jesus' prayer to the Father. Anyone who prays the Office of the Passion (OfP), written by him, prays, so to speak, like Christ Himself ("in persona Christi"). Therefore, Francis often added the words "Father" or "Holiest" or "Holy Father" to his own psalm verses. In these Psalms of Suffering Jesus becomes the self-declaration of man to God: "Look, this is the way man is!" and prays from us to his Father. In this way he becomes a mediator between God and man.

3. Psalm I (Compline) of the Office of the Passion and its interpretation

The Franciscan sources translate the text as follows:

*God, I have told you of my life; *
you have placed all my tears in your sight.

*All my enemies were plotting evil against me; *
they took counsel together.

*They repaid me evil for good *
and hatred for my love.

*They slandered me in return for my love, *
but I continued to pray.

*My holy Father, King of heaven and earth, do not leave
me *
for trouble is near and there is no one to help.

*Let my enemies be turned back on whatever day I shall call
upon you; *
for now I know that you are my God.

*My friends and my neighbours have drawn near and have
stood against me; *
those who were close to me have stayed far away.

You have driven my acquaintances far from me; *
they have made me an abomination to them. I have been
handed over and did not escape.

Holy Father, do not remove your help from me; *
my God, look to my aid.

Come to my help, *
Lord, God of my salvation.

Glory to the Father, and to the Son,
and to the Holy Spirit, *
As it was in the beginning, is now, and will be forever.
Amen.

P. Anton Rotzetter OFMCap (The Liturgy of the Hours of
St. Francis of Assisi, pp. 87-88) tries to translate the psalm
as follows for praying:

"God
I tell You about my life
You see:
my tears are flowing

All my enemies
have evil thoughts against me
They conspired against me
They answer with malice
to the good that I have done
And with hatred to my love
They attack me
instead of loving me
but I stand in prayer

My Holy Father
King of Heaven and Earth
do not leave me
Suffering and trouble are close to me
And nobody is there to help me

I know: You are my God
When I call You
my enemies retreat

My friends and my neighbors/loved ones
Betrayed me or left me alone
My neighbors
have stayed far away
You know
My friends do not want anything
to do with me
and curse me
I have been betrayed,
I am done for,
And there is no way out

Holy Father
Do not take Your helping hand
away from me
My God
look at me

Help me
Hurry to help me
Lord and God, my salvation."

This psalm meditation imagines Jesus' situation at the
Mount of Olives (betrayal and capture). The power of evil
becomes more palpable: tears, loneliness and
abandonment, then his arrest. In everything, the Lord
maintains an unshakable faith and unremitting prayer. In
verse three, the meaning behind this suffering becomes
evident: *for you*. Originally this psalm is to be prayed on
Maundy Thursday as part of Compline, the night prayer.

4. Exercise

A) As an exercise for this week, we shall be praying Psalm 1 of the Office of Passion (translation by P. Anton Rotzetter OFMCap or Franciscan Sources) again using the "Three steps of Franciscan Contemplation" (see introduction).

> ➤ I collect myself and perceive myself holistically. Then I place myself in the presence of Jesus and become aware of His gaze.
> I try to feel inside: How does He look at me in this Mount of Olives-situation? I look at Him and take part in His relationship with the Father.

> ➤ I read the psalm in connection with Jesus at the Mount of Olives and let Him speak to me.
> I imagine Jesus suffering and struggling and feel with Him.
> I seek communion with Him with the issues that surface from my own life.

> ➤ I release the will to understand and surrender myself to Him, who wants to embrace and involve me in His life. Let it be! Let it be!

It is possible to pray the same psalm throughout the week or to use other psalms from the Office of Passion for contemplation.

B) Another exercise during the week might be to connect His and my sufferings with each other through a deeper contemplation of the following picture.

Detail of the cross above the high altar,
Basilica of San Francesco, Arezzo

18. The Stations of the Cross

Introduction

This week we shall be delving into another Franciscan form of prayer: The stations of the Cross.
As an introduction to the topic I ask myself: Do I know the fourteen stations of the Cross? Is there a particular station of the Cross, which "comes to meet me" on my path of purification and promises salvation?

1. The history of the Stations of the Cross

The Stations of the Cross have their origins in the history of the Passion of Jesus, as recorded in the Gospels. In the Roman Empire, only slaves and people who did not have Roman citizenship were sentenced to death on the cross; the convict had to carry his cross to the place of execution himself. That is why the Gospel of John says: *"He (Jesus) went out, bearing his own cross, to the place called The Place of a Skull"* (Jn 19:17). One can trace the path that Jesus took and roughly localize it in Jerusalem. Thus, it is understandable that Christians have since wanted to walk on this path. According to an ancient tradition, shortly after the resurrection of Jesus, His mother Mary and the Jerusalem Christians followed the stations of His passion in the memory of their Lord.

At the beginning of the 4th century, memorial stones and chapels were erected above these sites, which are still now visited by pilgrims.
In the 12th century, the piety associated with of the stations of the Cross was deepened by the Crusaders and by Francis of Assisi (1182-1226). Francis, with the help of psalms, put together a literary way of the cross – his Office of the Passion. With these psalms he contemplated the suffering of Jesus every day. Similarly, a great veneration of Christ's

suffering is testified in the writings of St. Clare of Assisi (1193-1253) and her sisters.

From the 14th century onwards, the Franciscans accompanied pilgrims from all over the world on the path Jesus took from the court through the Via Dolorosa to the site of his execution at Golgotha.
In the West – influenced by medieval Passion mysticism, in southern Germany, for example through the Blessed Good Beth of Reute (1386-1420) – the Way of the Cross has been replicated since the 15th century, first in the open air (for example, Calvary Mountains), then increasingly in churches.
The greatest patron of the Way of the Cross was the Franciscan, Leonhard of Porto Maurizio (1676–1751). He built 576 stations of the cross during his numerous missionary journeys. He achieved that in 1731 Pope Clement XII. determined that the number of stations, which had hitherto not been fixed, should be fourteen.
During the last two centuries it has been the custom that in each parish, at least during Lent, the Way of the Cross is prayed in Franciscan monasteries, often every day of the working week.

2. The Way of the Cross in the life of St. Francis

As the Apostle Paul says, truly liberating belief shall grow in every Christian: *"I live in faith in the Son of God, Who loved me and gave Himself for me."* In contemplating the Passion of Christ and His resurrection, the believer recognizes himself as crucified with Christ and resurrected with Him: *"It is no longer I who live, but Christ who lives in me"* (Gal 2:20).

Francis of Assisi understands his life as a follower of the poor and humble Jesus, *"leaving you an example, so that you might follow in his steps"* (1 Peter 2:21).

He tried to copy the way of Jesus so radically that his body became Christ like through the stigmata. Francis was given the gift of suffering with his Lord in this community of love. In his praying and contemplation – as is evident in his Passions psalms – the focus is once on his being betrayed, then being taken prisoner and mocked, then tortured and convicted, on being abandoned and exalted on the cross, then on his dying and being resurrected – and on His absolute trust in His Father.

The legend of the three companions tells us how Francis once walked around crying at Portiuncula. When asked about the cause, he said, *"I lament about the suffering of my Lord Jesus Christ, for Whom I would not be ashamed to cross the whole world, lamenting loudly"* (3C 14).

Francis passionately invites all people to love as Christ loved – even one's enemies: *"Clear out of the way your willful self, and bear His holy cross, and obey His most sacred commandment until the end."*

This is how Francis leads us from contemplating the Lord suffering for us to concrete situations in our lives with suffering and tribulations, with sin and guilt. They are the place where we become transformed in Jesus Christ.

3. The Way of the Cross today

Today it is important to pay close attention to contemplating the Way of the Cross with love and experiencing its transformative effect in everyday life.

When walking the Way of the Cross and internalizing the images and events, the praying observer realizes the meaning of his own life, suffering and death – and that of his fellow human beings and the world.

He knows that everything finds its true place in the living presence of Christ, loved to the utmost and completed in hope. Thus, the Paschal Mystery becomes part of the present and shows us the way to the Father.

What was said nearly a millennium ago has a special immediacy for us today: *"But in order that the glow of the fire of love in man is not cooled by the constant consideration of injustice, he should always look with the eyes of the heart to the silent patience of his beloved Lord and Redeemer"* (Aelred of Rievaulx). Even when watching the daily news, with its frequent reports of horror and evil throughout the world, the contemplation of the Way of the Cross can have a healing effect and bring reconciliation to us and to the world.

4. Exercise

I look at one or more stations of the Way of the Cross every day.

I start with the preparatory prayer:

"Father, Your incarnate Son,
more beautiful than human children,
for the sake of my salvation
became the lowest of all people,
despised, broken and scourged all over his body
even died in the misery of the cross.
I want to contemplate Him, my Father,
I want to look upon Him,
I desire to imitate Him,
because He is my way to You."

(2LAg 2+3, formulated according to P. Helmut Schlegel)

> ➤ I settle down inwardly and externally and gather myself. I perceive the cross and Christ Crucified. I react to His gaze and let myself be gazed at.

➢ I pick a specific station of the cross, preferably one which resonates with me. I look at the station with the help of the text I have in front of me and "imagine" the situation with my inner eye with all the emotions it evokes.

➢ I let go of all thoughts and considerations and enter into communion with Jesus Christ, who is able to draw me into His life. I surrender to Him.

19. "Put yourself in front of the Mirror of Eternity"

Introduction

In the third letter to St. Agnes of Prague, (3LAg) the central teaching on prayer of St. Clare can be found. We owe this instruction to prayer to a request by Saint Agnes of Prague, who turns to St. Clare in personal darkness and prayer. St. Clare passes her own prayer experience on to her friend.

1. Text: 3 LAg 12-14.15b-17

Put your thoughts
in front of the mirror
of eternity.

Put your soul
in the brilliance
of glory.

Put your heart
in front of the picture
of the Being of God.

Let yourself be changed
and transformed in prayer
into the image of his deity.
You will feel
what His friends feel.
You will taste
the hidden sweetness,
which God has kept
from the beginning
for those who love Him.

With total dedication
give Him your love,
He, Who, abandoned Himself
with His whole being,
in order to love you,
He, Whose beauty
sun and moon admire,
He, Whose gifts
in their preciousness and magnitude
are without an end.

I mean Him,
the Son of the Most High,
Whom heaven and earth
are unable to fully grasp,
and Who nonetheless
in the womb of a human mother
allowed Himself to be formed and carried.

(Translation into contemporary language by Regis J.
Armstrong OFMCap)

2. Explanations of the interpretation

Clare shows in this letter a path of contemplation that is still helpful and valid today. Christian contemplation has two basic dynamics:

a) To stand completely in the presence of God:

- Let us first consider the thoughts, words and terms. In the "mirror of eternity", human thought is relativized. It gets the weight that it really deserves. At the same time, it becomes transparent giving access to deeper layers of being.

- The movements of the soul are our emotions, our temperament, our whole psychological make up.

Illuminated by the glory of God, they are purified and healed. In the encounter with God, all mental powers can be integrated into our ability to love.

- Finally, what matters is the immediate, intimate encounter with the essence of God. If God can touch and inhabit the "the center of our heart", we come to life from this innermost point (= soul, see 7th week) because we are "fed" with divine life. This permits is to taste God's presence as we surrender to him.

b) The second basic movement of contemplation is the dialogue with Christ:

This is a fluent giving and taking, being gifted and giving oneself. The praying person is gazed at by Christ and gazes at him. The relationship with Christ takes place less on the level of words than of gazing: the life of Jesus becomes the image that transforms us. It turns our entire existence into a sort of motherly womb that takes the being of Christ in and makes Him human.

3. Clare's concept of the "mirror"

In the fourth letter to Agnes of Prague (4LAg) Clare builds on her remarks of the "mirror" in the third letter with the following words:
"... since He is the radiance of eternal glory, is the brightness of eternal light and the mirror without blemish (Wis 7:26). Gaze upon that mirror each day, O Queen and Spouse of Jesus Christ, and continually study your face in it, that you may adorn yourself completely, within and without, covered and arrayed in splendour" (4LAg 14-16).

The mirror without blemish is Christ Jesus himself. Looking at the image of Christ, the "new man", I begin to

perceive and recognize myself better. Who am I when I look at myself from the perspective of Christ?
The ability for true self-knowledge only enables development of the self in the process of becoming whole.

Gazing requires stability. Not just looking every now and then, not when one feels the need or when it "suits" you, but constantly, every day. Consistent practice is needed because we use defense mechanisms that want to protect us from encounters, and from increased self-knowledge. Consistent gazing leads to awareness of the glory of the bridegroom.

The mirror contemplation is based on encounter and leads to examination of our knowledge of who we are and who we can be in front of Him. It is a question of holistic development of man in contemplation. The whole person is supposed to become "beautiful", internally and externally. When she uses the image of jewelry, Clare speaks as a woman, jewelry being an image for the new beauty that a person can achieve in the intimate encounter of being touched by God, which leads to holistic personal development. St. John of the Cross expresses this experience as follows:

> *"Do not reject me,*
> *because if You even encountered*
> *dark color inside me,*
> *you can still look at me now,*
> *because since You looked at me,*
> *You left love and beauty*
> *behind in me."*

4. Exercise

➢ Icons are a mirror of God for the Eastern Churches. Through the face of Jesus I am gazed at by the Triune God and myself gaze through the face of Jesus into the mystery of the Triune God.

➢ Look at the icon of the Cross of San Damiano, where St. Clare lived, or just look at the detail of the face of Christ Crucified of San Damiano.

➢ Or take another representation of Christ (perhaps your favorite Christ picture) and look at it daily using the "Three Steps of Franciscan Contemplation" (see introduction).

Cross of San Damiano, fragment

20. "See the Humility of God in the Holy Bread!"

Introduction

This week we are delving into the deep mystery of the Eucharist. Francis invites us to look in the power of the Holy Spirit: *"See, the humility of God!"* (in the Eucharist). – If we become silent with Francis, take an appropriate physical position and we "look" in communion with him through our spiritual senses, we will begin to grasp the great mystery of the constant incarnation of God among us.

1. Eucharist - a process of transformation which we are part of

Francis writes about the Eucharist more than anything else. In it the love of God becomes tangible. Yes, Francis feels embraced by the love of God. God descends into the abyss of his humanity, touching him there physically and carrying him body and soul, indeed with his whole being up into the glory of the Father. The celebration of the Eucharist is therefore not an external event for Francis, in which he simply watches what is happening or that he helps to celebrate. Rather, he is absorbed by the mystery of the Triune God when celebrating Holy Mass. God transforms the gifts of bread and wine in order to transform man. The Eucharist is a place of transformation and redemption. A few sentences from the "Letter to the Order" can help us to deepen this perspective of Francis'.

2. From the Letter to the Order (LtOrd)

- *"Kissing your feet, therefore, and with all that love of which I am capable, I implore all of you brothers to show all possible reverence and honor to the most holy Body and Blood of our Lord Jesus Christ in Whom that which is in heaven and on earth has been brought to peace and reconciled to almighty God."* (LtOrd 12-13).

- *"It is a great misery and a miserable weakness that when you have Him present in this way, you are concerned with anything else in the whole world!"* (LtOrd 25).

- *"Let everyone be struck with fear, let the whole world tremble, and let the heavens exult when Christ, the Son of the living God, is present on the altar in the hands of a priest! O wonderful loftiness and stupendous dignity!"* (LtOrd 26-27).

- *"O sublime humility! O humble sublimity! The Lord of the universe, God and the Son of God, so humbles Himself that for our salvation He hides Himself under an ordinary piece of bread!"* (LtOrd 27).

- *"Brothers, look at the humility of God, and pour out your hearts before Him! Humble yourselves that you may be exalted by Him!"* (LtOrd 28).

- *"Hold back nothing of yourselves for yourselves, that He Who gives Himself totally to you may receive you totally!"* (LtOrd 29).

3. Understanding the text

Francis wants to give the Lord great reverence and honor. Reverence means perceiving the physical reality of God in the smallness of bread and wine and respecting and honoring the presence of God.
God is there in His entirety. How can I think of something else when God gives Himself completely for me? He gazes at me and gives Himself to me without holding anything back. How should I not look at Him and not give myself to Him?

It is unbelievable that infinite, almighty God gives so much and lowers himself so that I become stronger than him. God surrenders to me completely in Jesus Christ, he gives Himself into my hands. I experience this in person in the Eucharist during communion: the Almighty lies defenceless in my hands. He is at my mercy, dependent on my actions, on everything I do. He even lets Himself be broken by my hands.
The Infinite asks me for a place in my little heart. He asks for shelter and dwelling in me. Can I put my joy into words?

God gives Himself in the form of bread, to be small enough so that I am not afraid and to be able to access my heart. Just as bread and wine are transformed into the body and blood of Jesus through the work of the Holy Spirit, my life is to be transformed into the reality of Jesus.

Most people today have great difficulty both with the word and with the ideal of humility.
The word humility is practically never used in public life. Who wants to be humble? However, God has become humble, says Francis, yes, he is humility himself. The Incarnation of humility present in the Eucharist. Humility is therefore not an ethical ideal, but following Christ. We can let ourselves fall into his humility. This humility of

God can be seen in the Eucharist and it can begin to transform us.

Because God gives Himself completely to me, gradually, step by step, I am able to give myself more and more to God. I no longer have to cling obsessively to myself and to my belongings, but can let go of everything in my movement towards God, and become poor because God Himself has become poor for me.

I am transformed in the praying union with God.

The Swiss patron saint, Brother Klaus prays in a similar way: "My Lord and my God, take me from myself and just give me completely to you."

4. Exercise

This week I will try to attend a celebration of the Eucharist as often or as prepared as possible. I prepare myself for the celebration with loving attention by internalizing the Eucharistic hymn of St. Francis from the letter to the order.

> ➢ I pray to the Holy Spirit to prepare me. Then I turn to the Eucharistic hymn and pray the whole text; then I let myself be led while ruminating.

> ➢ From His humility I "look" at myself and my current life, loving, suffering and hoping. In it I yearn and ask Jesus Christ in His eucharistic humility and poverty to be in me.

> ➢ I let go of myself with all previous experiences and images, including disappointments ... and I let His poverty and humility happen to me in accordance with his will.

21. "Welcome, my Sister Death!"

Introduction

Finally, at the end of this school of prayer, it is advisable to look at the end of St. Francis' and St. Clare's lives: on their deathbeds.
We are invited to become aware of our own dying, which is part of our life, and to prepare for it.

1. Francis and his death

Francis knew that his earthly life was coming to an end. Especially illness, stigmatization and conflicts in his order accompanied him on this painful last stage of his life.
He often confronted himself with his own end, sometimes every day; the "Day of Death" (AC 99: 9-10). As the day approached, he was carried into the chapel of Portiuncula. At the place where the order started, he wanted to end his poor life.
He wanted to die poor, lying on the ground, scattered with ashes in the circle of some brothers and had the Passion of the Lord in the Gospel of John read out to him. At his request, brothers sang to him the verse of "Sister Death" from the Canticle of the Sun, which the saint himself had written about two years earlier. So Francis invited death itself to praise God: "Welcome, my sister Death!" (AC 100:10; 2C 217:8)

The Canticle of the Sun

The Canticle of the Sun was written by Francis in the winter of 1224/25 when he was ill and resting in a hut in the garden of San Damiano. In his dejection, the Lord comforts him with the promise: "for your illness is the pledge of my Kingdom; by merit of your patience you can be firm and secure in expecting the inheritance of this

Kingdom" (2C 213,6). Thus, the canticle is the joyful answer to an experience of God in the dark night of the soul.

This prayer is not only a hymn to God's good creation, but it also challenges us in our behavior to the world and in the acceptance of sickness and the process of dying.

¹Most High, all-powerful, good Lord,
Yours are the praises, the glory, and the honor, and all blessing,
To You alone, Most High, do they belong,
and no human is worthy to mention Your name.

²Praised be You, my Lord,
with all Your creatures, especially Sir Brother Sun,
Who is the day and through whom You give us light.
And he is beautiful and radiant with great splendor; and bears a likeness of You, Most High One.

³Praised be You, my Lord, through Sister Moon and the stars, in heaven You formed them clear and precious and beautiful.
Praised be You, my Lord, through Brother Wind, and through the air, cloudy and serene, and every kind of weather, through whom You give sustenance to Your creatures.

⁴Praised be You, my Lord, through Sister Water,
who is very useful and humble and precious and chaste.

⁵Praised be You, my Lord, through Brother Fire,
through whom You light the night,
and he is beautiful and playful
and robust and strong.

⁶Praised be You, my Lord, through our Sister Mother Earth, who sustains and governs us,
and who produces various fruit
with colored flowers and herbs.

[7]Praised be You, my Lord, through those who give pardon for Your love,
and bear infirmity and tribulation.
Blessed are those who endure in peace
for by You, Most High, shall they be crowned

[8]Praised be You, my Lord, through our Sister Bodily Death, from whom no one living can escape.
Woe to those who die in mortal sin.

[9]Blessed are those whom death will find in Your most holy will, for the second death shall do them no harm.

[10]Praise and bless my Lord and give Him thanks and serve Him with great humility.

2. Clare and her death

Clare's last hours had come – she knew that. Contemporary witnesses tell us how Clare spoke to her soul: *"Go without anxiety", she said, "for you have a good escort for your journey. Go," she said, "for He Who created you has made you holy. And, always protecting you as a mother her child, He has loved you with a tender love."* (LegCl 46:1-4).

Clare walks consciously, courageously and decisively in the last stage of her life, trusting in God – just as she has hoped for him in her entire life. As a result, she experienced him as the one who now gives her soul security and good guidance. In her life of extreme poverty, she surrendered to the wealth of God all her life, thus daily. He didn't disappoint her; he sanctified her and always looked after her, like a mother looks after her child, and loved her with tender love.

And a last great praise is on her lips: *"May you be blessed, O Lord", she said, "You Who have created my soul!"*

(LegCl 46:5). Clare seems to have regretted nothing: poverty, illness, community life in strict enclosure – everything is integrated in God's reality, the God who created her and now leads her to eternal life.

3. Me and my own death

When we look at the dying of the two Saints, Francis and Clare, there are some similarities: dying in the presence of sisters/brothers; reading the Passion of Christ; prayer and praise; the ability to realize and pronounce that death has now come to "transitus" – the passage into eternal life ... Despite these similarities, the two Saints celebrate their deaths very personally.

I will die too, even if I don't think about it. No one can escape physical death alive. Fear and flight often make us avoid this reality.

"Ars moriendi" – the art of dying – has been spoken of since the Middle Ages. It seems that you can learn this "art" a little. Christian spirituality gives various recommenddations.

- The prayer for a blessed death; so that in death I can be counted among those blessed people who are found in God's most holy will.

- The daily night's rest can consciously serve as a "small school for dying": You lie down to sleep; will you wake up again? Everything that still surfaces unresolved in one can thus be surrendered to the redeeming love of God.

- Formulating evening and night prayers in this way can be very fruitful.

4. Exercise

A)

> Look at the Canticle of the Sun again and again; especially the 9th verse of "Sister Death". For Francis, his own praise is no longer enough; he invites all creation to praise God. Francis is reconciled to everything – everything has become brother or sister to him.
What prevents me from being in a constant inner state in which I can praise God?
- Where would I wish, if I had to die tomorrow, to have made peace and reconciliation beforehand?
- Which song would I like to sing to God while I am my dying?

> *"Blessed are those whom death will find in Your most holy will, for the second death shall do them no harm"* (CtC 9).
Just as Christ took on this first death, the disciple of Jesus can accept physical death in the hope that the resurrection of Christ will give him eternal life. For Francis, death is nothing but the passage to full communion with his beloved Lord. Through the death of Christ, death was transformed from being our enemy to being our brother/our sister.
I am again aware that nobody can escape physical death; but those whom he finds in God's most holy will, the second death will do no harm.

B)
I look at the death of St. Clare. For a long time already Clare was detached from the need and desire for possessions and prestige. For years she practised dying in everyday life. Clare is deeply reconciled to her life; she praises God for it without restriction.

➢ What prevents me from going to God?

➢ Are there still 'knots' in my life for which I cannot yet praise God, which I have not yet brought into contact with Him?

➢ Do I allow him to sanctify me, too?

➢ Do I trust him so that I can ask Him to be my last escort and can I be sure of this?

C)
I try to avoid the thought of my own death and take advantage of the many everyday opportunities to practise dying a little bit.

➢ How do I want to die? Am I in a state where I want to die one day? What else do I want to change?

➢ I try to offer a free prayer for a good death to God. (If necessary, write it down and pray it regularly.)

➢ When I go to bed in the evening, I deliberately surrender myself to God with all fears, with everything that is still unresolved – but also everything that has already been redeemed.

➢ And then there are countless possibilities, the "little deaths" in everyday life:

- to refrain from an angry word – even if I feel like I'm "suffocating" if I don't say it;

- to accept humiliation, insults and injustices, etc. it may cost me my reputation and my rights;

- to recognize and accept diseases and pain as messengers of transience (which does not exclude seeking medical help);

- just try to be in the will of God so that bodily death can meet me there
  Then it will come easily to me: *Welcome my sister death!*

D)
I pray and consider one of the following night prayers or prayers for a good death.

Night prayers

Take us good gracious Lord and God,
this night in Your care;
let us be safe in You:
In Your peace we can rest well.

While the tired limbs are resting,
our hearts shall keep turned to You.
We are Your people who trust You:
Protect us with a strong hand.

To you, God Father, Son and Spirit,
the calm of this night be dedicated.
When once the night of death surrounds us,
lead us into the light of glory. Amen.

(Hymn of Divine Office – Compline)

In the middle of life we are
embraced by death.
Who is it who brings us help,
that we can gain grace?
That is You alone, Lord.

We repent our iniquity,
which has angered you Lord.
Holy Lord God, Holy Strong God,
Holy Merciful Savior,
You Eternal God,
do not let us sink
into the bitter misery of death. Kyrie eleison.

(Hymn of Divine Office – Compline)

The earth already enfolds us
like a dark coat for the night.
Sleep, the gentle picture of death,
leads us to the grave of slumber.
When the black night encases us,
we are beset by dreams and delusion,
threatened by doubt and fear,
exposed to the power of evil.
Christ, You Life, Truth, Light,
watchful Guardian, be near us,
that faith may be watchful in us,
even in the dark time of sleep.
We ask Son and Father
and also the Spirit that unites both:
the Triune Power that guides everything
save us this night. Amen.

(Hymn of Divine Office – Compline)

Prayers for a good death

When it is time for me to leave,
then do not leave me.
If I should suffer death,
then You should stand by me.

If I am most terrified
in my heart,
tear me apart from the fears
through Your fears and pain.
Appear to me as a shield,
to comfort me in my death
and let me see Your image
Your misery on the Cross.
There I want to look at You,
there I want to hold You
faithfully tight to my heart.
Anyone who dies this way, dies well.
(Paul Gerhardt)
Oh, my Lord and Savior,
support me in that hour in the strong arms of Your
Sacraments,
and by the fresh fragrance of Your consolations.
Let the absolving words be said over me,
and the holy oil sign and seal me,
and Your own Body be my food,
and Your Blood my sprinkling;
and let my sweet Mother, Mary, breathe on me,
and my Angel whisper peace to me,
and my glorious Saints smile upon me;
that in them all, and through them all,
I may receive the gift of perseverance,
and die, as I desire to live,
in Your faith,
in Your Church,
in Your service,
and in Your love. Amen.
(Blessed Cardinal John Henry Newman)

Literature

Bonaventura, Breviloqium, (übertragen, eingeleitet und mit einem Glossar versehen von Marianne Schlosser / Christliche Meister 52) Freiburg i. Br. 2002

Bonaventura, Der Pilgerweg des Menschen zu Gott (übersetzt und erläutert von Marianne Schlosser), St. Ottilien [2]2010

Bonaventura, De triplici via / Über den dreifachen Weg (Übersetzung und Einleitung Marianne Schlosser), Freiburg i. Br. 1993

English source texts: https://www.franciscantradition.org

Gruber, Margareta / Mülling, Christina / Schneider, Herbert / Zahner, Paul (Hg.), Gottes-Sehnsucht. Einübungen in franziskanische Spiritualität, München 2005

Lehmann, Leonhard / Berg, Dieter (Hg.), Franziskusquellen. Die Schriften des heiligen Franziskus, Lebensbeschreibungen, Chroniken und Zeugnisse über ihn und seinen Orden (Band 1: Franziskus-Quellen), Kevelaer [2]2014

Leonhard Lehmann, Tiefe und Weite. Der universale Grundzug in den Gebeten des Franziskus von Assisi (Franziskanische Forschungen Heft 29), Werl 1984

Leclerc, Eligius, Weisheit eines Armen. Ein Jahr im Leben des Franz von Assisi, Kevelaer [2]2011

Rotzetter, Anton, Das Stundengebet des Franz von Assisi. Zum heutigen Beten neu erschlossen, Freiburg i. Br. 2002

Rotzetter, Anton / van Dijk, Willibrord-Christian /
Matura, Thadée (Hg.), Franz von Assisi. Ein Anfang und
was davon bleibt, Düsseldorf 2001

Schneider, Johannes / Zahner, Paul (Hg.), Klara-Quellen.
Die Schriften der heiligen Klara, Zeugnisse zu ihrem
Leben und ihrer Wirkungsgeschichte (Band 2: Klara-
Quellen), Kevelaer 2013

**Further English language documents for Franciscan
spirituality can be found here**:
Grundkurs zum Missionscharisma CCFMC
(www.franziskanisch.net)

Book references:

Christina Mülling

Gottes-Abstieg
Geistliche Gedichte
3. erweiterte Auflage 2017

Books on Demand, ISBN 9783739208244

Christina Mülling

Ich will leben
Gedichte die das Leben schrieb

Books on Demand, ISBN 9783743128460

Christina Mülling

Gottes-Schimmer
Geistliche Gedichte

Books on Demand, ISBN-10-3746055792

Christina Mülling

**Du wirst den Tod in uns wandeln in Licht: Den
Kreuzweg franziskanisch beten Gebundene Ausgabe**

Josef Fink Verlag, ISBN 978-3-89870-503-5

Christina Mülling und Paul Zahner

**IHM Wohnung und Bleibe bereiten:
Ein franziskanischer Exerzitienweg**

Books on Demand, ISBN-10 -3848204630

Die Psalmen

Mit Bildern von Sigmunda May und Meditationen von
Christina Mülling
Katholisches Bibelwerk, ISBN 978-3-460-32088-8